From Ballroom
to DanceSport

SUNY series on Sport, Culture, and Social Relations
CL Cole and Michael A. Messner, editors

SUNY series in Communication Studies
Dudley D. Cahn, editor

From Ballroom to DanceSport

Aesthetics, Athletics, and Body Culture

Caroline Joan S. Picart

State University of New York Press
Diane M. Halle Library
ENDICOTT COLLEGE
Beverly, MA 01915

Published by
State University of New York Press, Albany

© 2006 State University of New York

For information, address State University of New York Press,
194 Washington Avenue, Suite 305, Albany, NY 12210-2384

Production by Marilyn P. Semerad
Marketing by Fran Keneston

Library of Congress Cataloging-in-Publication Data

Picart, Caroline Joan, 1966–
    From ballroom to dancesport : aesthetics, athletics, and body culture / Caroline Joan S. Picart.
        p. cm. — (SUNY series on sport, culture, and social relations) (SUNY series in communication studies)
    Includes bibliographical references and index.
    ISBN 0-7914-6629-9 (hardcopy : alk. paper) — ISBN 0-7914-6630-2 (pbk. : alk. paper)   1. Ballroom dancing—Social aspects.   2. Popular culture.   I. Title.
    II. Series.   III. Series: SUNY series in communication studies

GV1746.P53 2005
793.38—dc22   2005001027

ISBN-13: 978-0-7914-6629-2 (hardcopy : alk. paper)
ISBN-13: 978-0-7914-6630-8 (pbk. : alk. paper)

10 9 8 7 6 5 4 3 2 1

Contents

Illustrations

Acknowledgments

I wish to thank the English department of Florida State University for allowing me a research leave in spring 2004, which enabled me to finish this project, as well as a Research and Creativity Award, which enabled me to travel and acquire necessary research materials. I owe a debt of thanks to several student assistants whose assistance in getting every little formatting and citation detail in place was invaluable: Caroline Burgess, Laura Pratt, Michael Goldsby, Erin DiCesare, Marietta Palgutt, Jodie Howard, Dan Funes, Donna Gallagher, Micah McMillan, Erin Irving, Chris Faupel, Andy Gately, John Browning, and Aimee Griffith. I also wish to extend my thanks to all my friends in dance, who have kindly answered my seemingly endless questions and endured numerous hours of interviews—without your help, the last two chapters of this book could not have been written. For the many times you have supported and cheered me on during performances and competitions, my gratitude is boundless. To the many ballroom teachers I have had—John Speros, Daniel Seguin, Gaspar Van der Ree, Mike and Dena Dill, and Shirley Johnson—many thanks for making these lessons rigorous, challenging, and fun. To my consistent dance partners, Mike Dill and Hubert Baxter, thanks so much for your commitment and professionalism but also for being enjoyable company during those long hours of practice and those all-too-brief moments of performance. To Carolyn Ellis, Art Bochner, and Norman Denzin, many thanks for encouraging me to explore an autoethnographic format to develop a distinctive voice in reflecting on my experiences as a competitor and student of ballroom dancing: that has opened many stimulating avenues for growth.

I am also deeply grateful to Carson Zullinger and Cecil Greek, who have been kind enough to authorize my use of their beautiful photographs in this book. Finally, I would also like to thank my family, and especially my mother, for detecting very early my passion for dance and cultivating it with ballet lessons, and then later Hawaiian and Philippine folk dance lessons. These acknowledgments would not be complete without a word of thanks to my husband, Davis Houck, whose understanding and generosity have been crucial to my carving out time for my twin passions of writing and dancing. Though he does not share my obsession with dance, being an academic, he does understand the importance of the life of the mind to me; and being a former All American golfer, he knows all too well the exhilaration and beauty of meaningful movement. We are two very different individuals shaped by two contrasting cultures, but we take turns leading and following, which perhaps explains why we have endured and grown together.

ONE

The Contested Landscape of Ballroom Dance

Culture, Gender, Race, Class, and Nationality in Performance

OVERALL CONTEXT AND FRAMEWORK

Two things prompt the writing of this book. First, there has been a resurgence in the popularity of ballroom dancing, as evidenced in the rapid incorporation of ballroom classes into physical education programs and the development of college scholarships; its incorporation into a boom of commercial films, such as the Australian *Strictly Ballroom* (1992), the Japanese *Shall We Dance?* (1996), the American *Dance with Me* (1998), the Spanish-Argentinean *Tango* (1998), and *Tango Lesson* (1997–1998), which involved a collaboration between the United Kingdom, Germany, the Netherlands, France, and Argentina; the incorporation of numerous regional, national, and international competitions into ubiquitous television entertainment; and the resurgence of ballroom dancing in nightclubs and ballroom studios as a valuable social asset. Second, there is increasing international anxiety over how (and whether) to transform ballroom into an Olympic sport, given that the change of status from being either a pastime or art into a serious sport also means an increase in commercial viability and prestige. Ballroom, and its sportier equivalent, DanceSport, are important to map because these constitute crucial sites upon which negotiations on how to package bodies as racialized, sexualized, nationalized, and classed are staged, reflective of larger social, political, and cultural tensions. More importantly, as ballroom/DanceSport continue to evolve in their choreography, costuming, and genre (such as the inclusion of more overtly balletic and gymnastic forms, exemplified in the cabaret or theatrical variety), these theatrical productions are aestheticized and constructed so as to encourage

1

commercial appeal, using the narrative frame of the competitive melo-drama to heighten audience interest.

Despite the plethora of how-to books on ballroom and a few theses on the topic (Carrie Stern's "Shall We Dance?: The Participant as Per-former/Spectator in Ballroom Dancing" and Mary Lyn Ball's "An Analysis of the Current Judging Methods Used in Competitive Ballroom, Including Comparisons to Competitive Pairs Figure Skating and Ice Dancing),[1] few critical manuscripts on ballroom have been published.[2]

Among the published books on ballroom dance and culture, Brenda Dixon Gottschild's *Waltzing in the Dark: African American Vaudeville and Race Politics in the Swing Era*[3] examines the social, racial, and artistic climate for African American performers from the late 1920s to the 1940s. While this book is valuable and instructive, it limits the notion of racial representation along the lines of an American black/white divide—something this book aims to problematize. Particularly with the growing international popular-ity of ballroom, the issue of race in relation to the politico-aesthetics of an evolving dance form is a complex phenomenon. Race, in this context, does not simply refer to American categorizations of blackness and whiteness, but also intersects with the notion of national identity, particularly as many of DanceSport's leading competitors and judges, even if they have emi-grated to the United States, are not American by birth.

Gerald Jonas's *Dancing: The Pleasure, Power and Art of Movement*,[4] views dance as a bodily language that expresses not only emotions or insights, but power as well. Its approach is mainly historical and ethnographic, and its use of vivid and well-placed photographs is effective for conveying the rich sociocultural underpinnings of these dances. It is, however, still very much a coffee table book and is meant as a general survey, moving across various African, Asian, Indian, and European dances. It has two chapters with sections on ballroom. Chapter 4, "Social Dance," deals with the rise of partner danc-ing and the cinematic success of the Fred Astaire-Ginger Rogers team; chapter 6, "New Worlds of Dance," focuses on the rise of the studio systems through the entrepreneurship of Vernon and Irene Castle and Arthur Murray, and the lindy hop and big band craze that fused the emphasis on pair dancing with the imperative to improvise or embellish a basic step with virtuoso improvisations. Though the book does draw from some auto-biographical observations or reflections by the author, these sections are brought in anecdotally, rather than as part of the theoretical apparatus of the book. In addition, ballroom is simply one among many dances of which the book attempts to draw a historical outline.

Julie Malnig's *Dancing Till Dawn: A Century of Exhibition Dance*[5] is principally a historical sketch of the increasing prestige of exhibition ball-room dancing from its heyday in the 1910s through the 1960s. It also uses primary sources such as promotional materials and print reviews, and is illustrated with original photographs. *From Ballroom to DanceSport*[6] would update this material and locate ballroom within a larger cultural context by drawing connections between the staging of ballroom as a potential Olympic sport, the return of its popularity as a social activity, and its ubiquity as a cinematic backdrop.

John Lawrence Reynolds's *Ballroom Dancing: The Romance, Rhythm and Style*[7] is informative in terms of its descriptions of ballroom's current status and its competition rules concerning steps and attire. Its use of colorful photographs reflective of current competitions enhances the book. However, it lacks a critical dimension and is more of a coffee table book than a critical text.

Dorothy A. Truex's *The Twenty Million Dollar Give-Away: An Expose of Competitive Ballroom Dancing*[8] is an expose of the seamier economic aspects of ballroom. What it does not do is provide a critical account that explains the appeal of ballroom, in spite of the huge financial costs it exacts from its enthusiasts; an analysis of its aesthetics and the elements of fantasy that motivate its practitioners reveals not only gendered, raced, classed, and sexualized aspects of the body, but also a sharp dichotomy between the aging body and the youthful body, and ties that in with similar issues within a broader politicocultural and economic context.

In general, each of these published academic books on ballroom have one or more of the following weaknesses that this manuscript seeks to avoid:

1. Some limit themselves to earlier periods of ballroom without addressing its more contemporary forms or its evolving contemporary significations. For example, Julie Malnig's *Dancing Till Dawn: A Century of Exhibition Ballroom Dance*, despite its many virtues, limits itself to an examination of the rise to prominence of exhibition ballroom dancing from 1890 through 1960.

2. Some, despite the wealth of contemporary information they provide, do not systematically critique the phenomenon. For example, John Lawrence Reynolds's *Ballroom Dancing: The Romance, Rhythm and Style* provides insightful descriptions of the two main styles of DanceSport, the American versus the English or European, along with their subdivisions, such as the standard and Latin dances, or the smooth and rhythm dances. Drawing from interviews with various contestants, displaying a practical knowledge of what judges value in competitions, and using photographs posed for the cameras during competitions or within photographic studios, the book provides a concrete and colorful glimpse into the world of ballroom.

However, it is mainly marketed as a coffee table edition, and as such, is descriptive rather than analytic.

3. Some focus on only one aspect of ballroom, without attempting to locate that aspect in relation to a larger, more complex terrain. One example is Dorothy A. Truex's *The Twenty Million Dollar Give-Away: An Expose of Competitive Ballroom Dancing*, which deals with the seamier side of ballroom as a business that encourages particularly older clientele to spend money beyond their means. Yet the critical analysis of the aesthetic and cultural dimensions of this phenomenon, which intersects with the enduring media popularity of ballroom, and its promotion of gendered, raced, classed, and sexualized ideals is not adequately developed.

4. Some deal with the racialized aspects of ballroom, but do so in a very limited way. For example, Brenda Dixon Gottschild's *Waltzing in the Dark: African American Vaudeville and Race Politics in the Swing Era* focuses on the social, racial, and artistic milieu within which African American performers worked during the swing era, from the 1920s to the 1940s. While this work is of immense scholarly value, it does not deal with more contemporary settings, and its reduction of racial issues to African American representation alone does not reflect ballroom's/DanceSport's cosmopolitan appeal or its transnationality as both a social and athletic phenomenon.

In contrast, the following are a few distinctive features of this book:

1. It draws from what Bruno Latour calls the "hot" sites within which ballroom's image is being rhetorically shaped. These include corporately sponsored ballroom magazines such as *DanceSport Magazine*; magazine-newsletters run by amateur associations such as the United States Amateur Ballroom Dancers Association's *Amateur Dancers*; websites run by both professional and amateur associations and individuals; local, national, and international televised competitions; and fashion magazines and websites that peddle ballroom apparel, jewelry, shoes, and other items.

2. It examines ballroom's current international popularity as a mise-en-scène upon which cinematic stories about gender, race, class, sexuality, power, and identity are forged.

3. As part of the examination of media and cinematic images of ballroom, it integrates relevant frame grabs or camera-ready photographs from competitions, fashion ads, professional announcements, and films.

4. It incorporates contemporary interviews with actual competitors, social dancers, teachers, and judges.

5. Parts of it will employ an autoethnographic or autobiographical format, which draws from my own experiences as a competitor and student of ballroom. I was initially trained in ballet, Hawaiian, and Philippine folk dance in the Philippines and then moved on to being trained in the English ballroom style at Cambridge, England, in 1990. I have been retrained in the American ballroom style since 1997.

6. Unlike other books that often limit themselves to one approach, which is usually historical in nature, this manuscript draws from an interdisciplinary approach, incorporating not only a strictly historical timeline, but also sociological, ethnographic, rhetorical, feminist, and critical and cultural studies frameworks.

The emphasis of the book is principally rhetorical, which means its key focus is on arguments being made, whether explicitly, in the form of outright verbal pronouncements or press releases, or implicitly, in the way bodies are clothed or framed or shot. The fulcrum of the book is how ballroom dancing is symbolically constructed and understood by different audiences. Both the symbolic construction and how audiences understand symbolic constructions constitute the realm of rhetoric.[9] Ballroom dance, and its competitive Olympic equivalent, does and should have multiple meanings to the multiple audiences I study (which include self, significant others, experts, competitors, viewers of films, and sports fans, among others). The Olympic exigence calls for a careful analysis of the emerging global presence of ballroom dancing and the attempt by some to transform it into a sport, which is dominated by heterosexual, agonistic assumptions. In addition to examining the Olympic conundrum, I also explore several experimental breaks with the drive toward the dream of Olympic inclusion as a full sport (with its underpinning global capitalist structures). Ultimately, a major aim is to chart the ambivalent gains— the dangers and potentials of transforming ballroom dance into a sport, and the power of alternative and inventive modes of dance that are currently underexplored. The Olympic controversy is the final topic the book deals with, but it is but one of several strands that flow from the central argument concerning the multiple meanings generated by dance performance. The "art versus sport" question thus serves as a central touchstone designed to illustrate the global importance of the topics this book is concerned with, but would not diminish the importance of more autobiographically rooted and local insider insights.

Thus, in the last chapters of the book, though some attention is paid to the time line in the official progress toward the achievement of Olympic status, such as in the minutes or press releases produced by the United States Amateur Ballroom Dance Association or the International Olympic Committee, this book goes beyond these often drab and sometimes legalistic documents. Before then, however, to understand how ballroom has become successfully poised to metamorphose into its competitive, athletic form, DanceSport, one must chart some of the larger cultural phenomena influencing and enabling this transformation. To do that, one must sketch, to the extent possible, the outlines of how ballroom dance has now become part club dance and part gym substitute, and, as depicted in movies, music, and advertising, a glamorous activity. Ballroom dance thus becomes the template for values concerning masculinity and femininity, whiteness and nonwhiteness, heterosexuality and homosexuality, nationalism and xenophobia, among others. The look of what is properly sporty or arty involves a complex set of negotiations in which these traditional binary dichotomies are both reinforced, but also rendered more fluid. Thus, men who dance ballroom are often overdetermined as "men" in their costuming, but they are also required to look graceful; women are similarly hyperfeminized in their modes of dress and make-up, but are required to hold their own in terms of physical stamina and power. It is these complex rhetorical "dances" that this book charts, rather than simple time lines. Even more fundamentally, the book also flows from my perspective as an "insider-outsider" to ballroom dance—as both one of its practitioners, but also one of its critics—and it is important to begin there.

WATCHER AND WATCHED: INSIDENESS AND OUTSIDENESS IN LIVING, WRITING, AND THEORIZING THE BALLROOM DANCER'S BODY

Paul Stoller, in *Sensuous Scholarship*, wrote of the need to "reawaken profoundly the scholar's body by demonstrating how the fusion of the intelligible and the sensible can be applied to scholarly practices and representations."[10] This chapter follows that ethnographic aim, focusing on the movement across the realms of private and public bodies, of the intellectual and the physical, of the watcher and watched—which are crucial to the apprenticeship and practice of ballroom dance. Thus, this chapter is an attempt to document the larger social backdrop within which DanceSport's bid to be an Olympic sport is grounded.

A crucial dimension of the approach I take in this chapter is the concept of the insider-outsider because dance does entail movement across different layers of "insideness" and "outsideness."[11] The concept of being an insider-outsider is derived from Maria Lugones's vision of the "new mestiza consciousness," which in turn is born from the complex interplay between oppression and resistance, where resistance is understood as a social and collective activity. *Mestizaje*, as she characterizes it, is marked by "the development of tolerance for contradiction and ambiguity, by the transgression of rigid conceptual boundaries, and by the creative breaking of a unitary aspect of new and old paradigms."[12] In Lugones's reading of Gloria Anzaldua's *Borderlands/La Frontera*,[13] which deals with the psychology of oppression, she imagines a consciousness that resists dualistic thinking, and acknowledges the need for racial, ideological, cultural, and biological "cross-pollination" in order for Chicanas and other women of color to remain self-critical and self-animated pluralities rather than "hyphenated being[s], . . . dual [personalities] enacted from the outside, without the ability to fashion [their] own responses."[14]

Lugones's terminology is instructive because it gets at the politico-cultural chiaroscuro of inside-outsideness I live. I occupy the liminal realm of the mestiza and the metaphorical cyborg materially. I am Filipino by birth, but my family is of mixed ancestry: my father has French American roots, and my mother, a hint of Spanish Chinese blood. But I also inhabit this in-between space professionally as a trained molecular embryologist and philosopher, and semiprofessional visual artist and ballroom dancer.

Though I have been a student of several dance forms (ballet, Philippine folk dance, Hawaiian dancing as filtered through a Filipino lens, and the Korean dance of exorcism known as *salpuri*), what follows is a montage of reflections on the nature of gendered and embodied interaction principally focused on ballroom dances, seen through different narrative lenses, allowing, once again, a fluctuation across insider and outsider perspectives. The focus on ballroom is crucial because it provides a prism through which issues of what differentiates studio culture from social opportunities for dancing may be filtered. Furthermore, ballroom, as a popular pastime now evolving into a potential Olympic medaled event, DanceSport, is voracious in its assimilation of stylized cultural and bodily habits. Thus, it provides a useful locus through which one may plot, for example, the bodily imprints of other dances, such as ballet (which has its own studio culture), and its more ethnic counterparts, such as the Tango of Argentina or the Samba of Brazil. Thus, whenever an analogy or a comparison between the various ballroom dances and these other dances I have studied proves useful for illustrating a point, I juxtapose these different realms of bodies and meanings. Nevertheless, for the purpose of creating a more readily readable text, I have chosen to keep the main focus on ballroom dance. As I show, issues of femininity and masculinity, being subject-objects of the aesthetic gaze, and issues of freedom and constraint are paramount to the exploration of what it means to do ballroom as both a competitive event and an art form.[15] Being someone who has apprenticed and competed in, and yet continues to be a student of ballroom dance, once again provides me with multiple perspectives. As someone who both leads (that is, steps into the traditionally masculine role) and follows (steps into the traditionally feminine role) both in social and performative contexts, I am able to explore or experiment with what it means to create masculine or feminine lines. Thus, I am particularly interested in what it means to communicate clear bodily cues, such that the person I am dancing with can adjust easily to these (which leading entails), or to be sensitively attuned, every muscle and nerve alert, for the slightest cue, so that two separate bodies may move in unison (which following requires). As someone who is part of ballroom studio culture, and as someone who dances in purely social contexts, I move across a host of varying cultural expectations, because studio dancing and social dancing have very different rules, just as dancing the waltz with a country dancer is very different from dancing the waltz with a ballroom dancer.

I examine how ballroom dance is created and taught, and how the highly codified steps and styles are integrated with the need to constantly recreate the structure of each dance performed. I wondered how different bodies, levels of skill, and styles adapt to each other. I was also curious about the process by which everyday people became performers in the context of the social hall, club, or ballroom studio, and wondered what motivated people to dance, both socially and competitively. I found myself intrigued by the etiquette of the dance floor and how it is affected by social interactions off that floor. I found myself fascinated by the role of dancing in the development of an actual romance, as well as the aesthetic romance of dancing. I asked how watchers judge what they see. With these questions, I have explored the unusual way in which all ballroom dancers occupy both the watcher and the dancer roles, and their methods for smoothly switching across these roles.

The physical knowledge I gained as I began to participate helped me interpret other dancers' views through data gathered both in interviews and from articles about ballroom dancing. Experience helped me discuss dancing comfortably and authoritatively with practitioners, and helped me to structure questions that caused dancers to think about their kinesthetic experiences. At times the information gained in these ways affirmed my experience and observations; equally as often it caused me to rethink and reexamine them. In a sense, other bodies clarified, expanded, confirmed, and questioned the knowledge my own body was gathering. This project, then, reflects the kinesthetic experiences of many bodies, my own and those of the people I interviewed, watched, and read about, privileging both what was said or reported, and what was seen and felt. The "field notes" for this book include interviews with other participants, both students and teachers, with whom I shared various points of convergence—as an advanced student who also teaches part-time. Extended conversations with me—or written interviews responded to in depth—provided some dancers with an opportunity to reflect on things they often took for granted. My questions, though carefully choreographed, once asked often set up a discussion that ricocheted far from my original intent, and I have rearranged the material to allow the flow of the dancers' voices to correspond with my own phenomenological reflections on my dance biography—how different types of dances have impressed themselves into my bodily memory, leaving imprints, once again gifting me with an insider-outsider perspective, which can be both illuminating and debilitating.

Thus, the method I used in my interviews intersects with Brenda Dixon Gottschild's imperative regarding participant/researcher dialogue that context, being fluid, should suggest an adaptable methodology.[16] Thus, I welcomed all responses and encouraged informants involved in this research project to disagree with me, when they could. More often than not, the participants who disagreed tended to be older white men, though one Hispanic man in his twenties expressed similar views concerning the politics of gender in ballroom. Often they pointed out or explained aspects of performance or of society that they felt I had misunderstood. Some used that opportunity to express their own philosophies and theories about dancing in general, and ballroom dancing in particular.

Writers from several disciplines have helped me forge a vocabulary and set of theoretical frames concerning the social and performance aspects of the ballroom event. Sociologist Elizabeth Burns's *Theatricality: A Study of Convention in the Theatre and in Social Life*[17] helped to formulate issues of stagelike behavior in a social performance. The work of sociologist Erving Goffman[18] has been useful in my examination of the social aspects of ballroom society. Yet perhaps the most crucial has been the return to the physical body of the researcher, advocated emphatically by particularly movement scholars, from many fields. Among those whose work helped in my formulation of the insider-outsider position in ballroom dance include Barbara Browning, Jane Cowan, Diane Freedman, Sally Ann Ness, and Cynthia Cohen Bull, who are all movement scholars employing different methodologies.[19] In addition, two anthropologists, James Clifford and Michael Jackson, were also influential in their convergence with the phenomenological stress on the importance of lived experience.[20] All these methodologies combine to buttress the autoethnographic exploration of the insider-outsider position in relation to ballroom dance that I enact in this chapter.

MEMOIR OF A DANCER:
THE PHILIPPINES AND SOUTH KOREA

I began ballroom dancing in 1991, desiring to get away from the intellectual intensity of working on a PhD in molecular embryology, and the emotional exhaustion of having broken up with the first man I had ever conceived of marrying—a young Belgian with perennial health problems and a burning ambition to be a diplomat, both of which proved incompatible with the fifteen-hour days I tended to spend at the laboratory and my own professional aspirations. Cambridge University certainly did not lack for social outlets, and I decided I needed to return to the main physical activity that had sustained me in my younger years: dance.

My love affair with dance began when I was about four years old. My mother had hired a nun at a nearby convent as a piano teacher for myself and my brother; she found that we took to piano instruction better (that is, in a more docile, obedient fashion) if we took lessons from someone else. Yet the nuns who ran the convent were quite ambitious, and every time they had their yearly recitals, they required that the students do more than play the piano. We were also required to recite poetry and to perform dances ranging from ballet to Hawaiian hula dances. I remember, in particular, one ballet dance number that required five young girls in formation, and I ended up being the soloist at a crucial point of the dance. We were all required to wear white dresses and crowns, to give the dance its required ethereal character. I remember being so nervous during the piano duet I played with my mother before the dance number that my hands were icy and shaking; she gave my hands the usual gentle squeeze, and somehow I survived the ordeal. I sailed through the dance number in a dreamlike haze. My mother proudly told me I did very well, and then remarked thoughtfully that it was time I stopped wearing those dark brown shorts underneath my skirt. It turns out that at the crucial point of the solo routine, as I lifted my arms in the arabesque position, my skirt lifted to reveal my tomboyish shorts (that is, the shorts with which I could scale trees and play war games with my brother and his friends), to the amusement of the audience.

As I stepped into the large gym in which the ballroom classes were held, I remember being a little nervous. Most people taking the classes were undergraduates; though I could pass as an undergraduate (thus making me an insider of sorts), very few international students were there. There were a handful of Indians or Pakistanis, but the majority were British and seemed to have the standard cliques. But once the dancing started, these divisions seemed to melt in the absorption of learning steps, moving in time to the music, and coordinating our movements with various partners. I found that Austrian and Spanish men seemed much more at ease with partner dancing, partly because dancing was an active part of their cultures. British men, on the other hand, seemed almost afraid of partner contact and were a little more stiff if they were beginners. Spanish men were famous for and much desired for their "Latin hips;" Austrian men were masterful, particularly with the Viennese waltz, with its numerous turns, and especially as many of them did not see dancing the waltz as a threat to their masculinity, but in fact, enhanced it.

I had my first dance competition in December 1990. I remember the excitement of preparing for the event; in some ways, it was like a throwback to high school. Once again, there was a lot of excitement and anxiety over finding the right partner. I sensed that for many of the younger people, finding the right partner also meant hopefully dating them afterward. Since I had begun dancing with the I-don't-want-to-complicate-my-life attitude, I had a relatively easier time. The dance teachers simply paired off single men and women randomly, and perhaps unsurprisingly, I ended up with a young Indian man as a dance partner.

The contest in itself was instructive. It commenced with the beginners, and my partner and I excitedly joined the crowded floor. Numbers were pinned to the men's backs so that couples could be easily identified. The only criterion that I remember being cited was keeping time with the music. My partner and I were doing quite well on the cha-cha and had our friends cheering when he missed one beat, and we were rapidly marched off the floor. He apologized profusely; I simply smiled, and proceeded to watch, with great interest, as the more advanced dancers took the floor. I remember being particularly struck with how diaphanous and revealing the Latin dance women's costumes were, and wondered if I would ever be comfortable wearing those costumes.

SEOUL, SOUTH KOREA
FEBRUARY 1993

"No, no beautiful!" Miss Yon, my *salpuri* dance instructor, half moans and half giggles at the same time.[21] (*Salpuri* is a traditional Korean dance, originally performed as a dance of exorcism by priests, who are traditionally male. It consists of a powerful, yet lyrical series of motions in which the dancer at times seems to float or tread upon invisible water.)

"Look me," she commands as she takes slow mincing steps in front of the single mirror in the room. Her feet alternately rise on the rounded parts of her toes (not on the tips, as ballerinas do) and slide back to rest upon slightly elevated ankles.

I stare and frown.

"See, no water," she says, mimicking what I have just done: rising to the tips of my toes in the characteristic balletic fashion and neatly taking rapid, sharply pointed steps. "Look, water." Holding me with her eyes, she again executes the same rocking, lingering, semielevated steps that make her look as if she is treading upon the surface of water.

Learning a new dance is like stepping into a new body, I think as I study her movements. Suddenly, it is no longer a matter of course to rise on one's toes and to plié, knees spread outward forming mirror images of each other. So much of dance entails doing violence to certain habits that clothe and contour one's body and the way one moves. Each dance form simply requires a different sense of physicality.

I have no choice but to try to break down fluid motion into a series of incremental movements. It is as if I were trying, mentally, to construct a cartoon version of a movement in real life. My body reflects that jerky, celluloid mimicry of the real that fluctuates between the funny, the awkward, the clumsy, and what has been called "charming" by kinder souls. I shake my head. Steeling myself, I try to execute the movements in a more fluid and less self-conscious manner.

"Good." Miss Yon's dark eyes sparkle. "Next learn."

She takes a silk scarf and grabs one end. Measuring about a foot from the edge, she inserts the cloth between the second and third fingers of her right hand, moves along the cloth till she reaches the other end, estimates what is approximately the same distance from that end and lets the section of the cloth hang between her thumb and second finger, returns to the first cloth border and brings it over her third and fourth fingers to lie between her fourth and fifth fingers. I immediately follow suit with little difficulty.

Learning to use it, though, is no simple matter.

"No, pfinger only." Miss Yon immediately catches an error. "No move!" She grasps my arms firmly. "Pfinger only." She pauses for a moment. "And no hip move. Body, no hip." I realize, with a sinking feeling, that even my training in Hawaiian and Latin American dancing will have to be held in check. The free and subtly sensual wavelike motions of the arms and hips, too, would have to be carefully suppressed, albeit momentarily. Each dance form has its own cultural identity, and imprints itself onto the flesh of the dancer who dares to attempt to master it, and eventually, be mastered by it. To me, the ultimate act for a dancer is one of surrender. A true dancer allows a dance form to dance itself out, using every trembling muscle or screaming nerve; every rise and fall of the breast; every tilt of the head or movement of the eye.

At first I hold my arms and hips stiffly, as if they are enclosed in girdles of iron. Then, as I watch Miss Yon, I realize that in place of the swaying of the arms, a subtle movement of the shoulders and the torso creates a similar, but more restrained visual effect: in place of the swaying hip movement, a slightly rotating upper torso combined with the semielevated steps of the feet enable one to achieve different forms of bodily alignment. This, too, creates an image of fluidity and achieves a different form of beauty.

"Kay," Miss Yon's voice is gentle. "Respire. Deep breath. One, two. Three, four. One, two. Three, four."

As I breathe deeply in unison with her, I realize that this cadence and degree of inhaling and exhaling allows me not only to enter more spontaneously into the rhythm of this dance form, but also to assume its various positions and movements.

MOVING INTO THE U.S.

After Korea, finding outlets for dancing ballroom proved challenging. At Penn State University, I was invited to be part of an elite group of lead dancers at the university ballroom club, but once again, finding a partner with whom to dance regularly proved challenging. Men who liked to dance and were good at it were often already paired with women who, understandably, guarded that alliance jealously. During our courtship days, my husband Davis took one ballroom class with me at a small studio close to campus, but it became clear to both of us that this was not an activity he spontaneously enjoyed. When I moved to the University of Wisconsin-Eau Claire in 1997, I immediately took part in the activities of the UWEC Ballroom Club, and was soon thereafter recruited as an advisor. 1997–98 proved to be a period of great popularity for ballroom on campus. Every semester, on the first day the organization convened, five hundred students showed up, causing the student instructors to have to harness another nearby room, which was not always the best for dancing; that other room often proved to be the location where martial arts and gymnastics classes were held, and consequently, its floors were padded. But because there seemed to be a great demand for swing and its acrobatics, that turned out to be a good safety measure. Hardly an environment for polishing technique, but most students were out there simply to expend energy and to move vigorously to music. Apparently, the Gap khaki commercials, with their catchy music and breathtaking, energetic lifts, had helped spark a craze, and for the two years that I was there, everything from male gigolo outfits with their long gold chains to swing polka-dotted balloon skirts flourished. Since the Twin Cities, Minneapolis-St. Paul, were only about an hour and a half away (depending on the snowfall and other weather conditions), a small group would occasionally carpool for a weekend in order to get to various swing clubs, dance vigorously until the clubs shut down at about one o'clock in the morning (unlike Latin clubs, which would go on all night), proceed to an all-night breakfast place, wolf down what seemed like an enormous amount of food, head for the hotel, shower, and then crash in shared rooms in order to cut on costs. I was the only professor who came along during these stints, but because of my slight stature, I tended to camouflage quite well. I found that having that insider-outsider position (passing as an undergraduate while being a professor on a first-name basis with chosen students) often buffered a lot of potentially awkward situations—undergraduates knew I was there to dance and to share in the physical expenditure and exhiliration of that experience, and treated me with a unique blend of deference and camaraderie. Though many of them called me "Kay," perhaps it was the "Minnesota niceness" that kept the lines clear.

I continued to take lessons at a small electic dance studio, whose dances ranged from ballet, modern, and tap, to ballroom, and continued to go social dancing in groups at several affairs held by the local Elks' Club, with a few stints to "the cities" for United States Amateur Ballroom Dancers Association (USABDA) affairs. I also started performing ballroom numbers with my teacher, Jerry, at local dance concerts and at the university, enjoying the rigor of collaborating on choreographing routines and the slight tension that came with performing. At such times, I came to realize the enormity of the responsibility of leading, because when Jerry failed to remember a series of steps, I would have to surrender to his lead and simply wait until he remembered where to pick up the choreographed sequence. Since I tended to remember the sequence more, we developed the survival tactic of whispering code words to each other (with me thus verbally taking over the lead, while appearing not to), through clenched, smiling teeth, of what steps followed next, while performing, in order to keep unpredictabilities to a minimum.

In January 1998 I finally caved in to curiosity and walked into my first Arthur Murray studio as a student, taking advantage of their advertised first free lesson. My principal motivation for doing so was simply the desire to get better, particularly in terms of technique. I had seen other studio-trained dancers dominate the floor during various social occasions in the cities, and I wanted to learn how to move like that. I found out very quickly that the community at the studio and its ethos were very different from the other dance circles in which I concurrently participated. Most of the people taking ballroom lessons at Arthur Murray tended to be young professionals (often in their thirties and older) who belonged to a certain economic class and level of education, as evidenced in their dress and demeanor. The university ballroom club, hardly surprisingly, tended to attract predominantly undergraduates, with only a handful of faculty or staff members. The other studio in which I now cotaught tended to attract people in their thirties as well, but they, unlike the Arthur Murray crowd, were more heterogenous in dress and manner of interaction.

Other ballroom dance students have told me interesting stories about why they first stepped into the Arthur Murray studio for the first time. Leonard Elzie, a fifty-eight-year-old economist, humorously recounted, "I asked a girl to dance. About two or three measures into the song, she stopped and looked at me and said, 'You really can't dance, can you?' So the next day, I went to Arthur Murray to learn how. That was about 15 years ago."[22] Sara Hurst, a forty-nine-year-old veterinary office manager and former medical technologist, said: "After being divorced, another friend and I were looking for a safe, smoke-free environment to meet people. . . . I was hooked immediately."[23]

My first lesson involved meeting my teacher-to-be, John Speros, who also turned out to be the owner of the studio, and explaining my dance history. We then proceeded into introductory steps in a number of dances, ranging from the foxtrot and waltz to the cha-cha and the swing. Since John saw that I knew a fair bit and could instinctively follow, he began stressing foxtrot technique on the very first day. The first thing I learned was to take a "heel lead" and "peel off" the front part of my foot as I walked backwards in closed dance position. Never had walking seemed so complicated. Through all of this, John kept a steady stream of conversation going, and I quickly learned that to survive in this setting, particularly during practice parties, one had to learn how to converse and dance at the same time, while also navigating the flow of human bodies moving across a crowded dance floor— and hopefully never stopping, missing a step, or crashing into someone.

Old-world etiquette was an integral part of studio culture. During group classes, we were always encouraged to clap our hands in appreciation of our partners, regardless of whether or not the step was accomplished correctly and with perfect precision, before we rotated on to the next partner. At parties, though both sexes could freely mingle and seek out partners as the next piece of music would be announced, gentlemen were expected particularly to thank their partners and escort them back to their seats, and ladies to be gracious about having been asked to dance. Unlike club dancing, where some men took advantage of the situation for inappropriate intimate contact, decorum strictly demanded that no such exploitative behavior occur, particularly between teachers and students. If a newcomer looked like he was being predatorial towards women, often a male teacher would cut in. Women, regardless of the level of expertise of the men, were expected to follow the man's lead, even if the man was dancing completely off-beat, which often happened with the mambo, since "breaking" or moving on the second beat was not easy.

STUDIO LIFE

When I asked several students at the studio at which I took lessons to reflect on the gender politics of leading and following, I got a broad range of responses. Fred Roberson, a database administrator, laconically replied that he did not reflect much on this at all. His wife, Anna, a teacher and school counselor, confessed that occasionally, "when the leader doesn't feel the music, I want to lead." Ann Mock, a receptionist, diplomatically replied that she thought "both roles [leading and following] are equally important," but her husband, David Mock, a history instructor, had a lot more to say: "The fact that the man leads is NOT gender politics. Someone has to lead. . . . It has nothing to do with 'gender politics.' And do I think of it? Of course not. I'm too concerned about keeping my partner from being creamed by someone who is going against the line of dance or who is going to do some snazzy step that takes four times the amount of available room."[24] Irene Padavic, a professor, delivered a rebuttal to David Mock's sharp rejoinder: "I think about it all right, and I find it anachronistic and annoying. It's one reason I prefer international folk dance. By the way, dancers in that genre simply quietly did away with the male-dominated elements when this style became popular in the 1970s (it need not be a man at the head of the line now, both sexes dance in lines that were single-sex in the old country, etc.). I don't know why they survive intact in the ballroom community."[25]

A number of women, including Pat Erdman, a seventy-nine-year-old retired judicial assistant to the Florida Supreme Court, interpreted the question to be asking whether she minded dancing with women instructors (since statistically, women, both as instructors and students, still outnumber the men, about four to one) and replied, "Women instructors are very good and I don't mind dancing with them informally."[26] Eloise Harbeson, a seventy-six-year-old retired director of library services at Tallahassee Community College, echoed Pat's remarks and added that she thought of ballroom as a sport and therefore thought that everyone, as part of a team, had a part to play. Ron Hancock, a sixty-six-year-old civil engineer, replied, "In our society, it is easier if the man leads and the woman follows. Each is quite difficult and necessary for ballroom."[27]

Yet trading places, for most people, is not an easy thing to do. It is not simply a matter of committing, to muscle memory more than cognitive memory, the timing and the oppositional correlatives of the patterns of steps of the various dances. More than that, it entails, in effect, an entire personality change. Most leaders become accustomed to occupying the role of being the brain or the general of the operation—planning ahead, taking the initiative, being decisive. Most followers acclimate to the "mirror-imaging" condition—remaining open and sensitively attuned, responding only when prompted, resisting the urge to think that one knows exactly which step is coming next before the cue comes.

Interestingly, questions concerning possible racial and class depictions implicit in the different dances, or the histories of the dances, did not raise an animated set of responses. Most students who came to the studio tended to be pragmatists and remarked that they had never really thought much about these, or that though the histories were interesting, they were essentially irrelevant to learning how to dance. Their responses tended to mark me as an outsider—perhaps even one who threatened to lessen the amount of enjoyment they derived from ballroom by raising questions concerning its depictions of race and class. Tricia Kiser remarked, "To me, dancing is an interpretive art form in which you perform a role. You act snobby and snooty for the Tango, formal and aristocratic for the Waltz and so on, but I don't see it as a commentary on a particular race or class."[28] The irrepressible David Mock effectively turned the question on its head by responding, "What *are* the 'implicit depictions of race and class in ballroom'? That most blacks and most poor people don't like ballroom dancing? . . . There's nothing that keeps anyone from ballroom dancing. There are lessons at FSU [Florida State University] that are $5 a semester, but the racial and socio-economic picture is the same there as at Arthur Murray's or the American Legion on Tuesday nights. What about *ageism*? Most of the people who ballroom dance are old."[29] Irene Padavic gave as balanced and empirical a response as possible, given her background as a sociologist: "In Tallahassee, the majority of ballroom dancers are working- or lower-middle class, in my observation. So there seems to be no sense here that it's for elites. As for race, I think I have never seen a non-white man. Non-white women are somewhat more common, although the two times I have seen black women at my regular ballroom dance they never returned."[30]

One of the first things I learned about studio culture at Eau Claire was that one had to be very careful, particularly in negotiating that student-teacher relationship. Despite the no fraternization rule within the Arthur Murray system, I was told that older single women, in particular, tended to fall in love with their instructors, and jealously guarded their "territory." A male instructor who became a friend told me how, in the past, all instructors were required to have studio names (as opposed to their real names) in order to prevent students from finding out where they lived and in effect stalking them. He also confided that there was once an older woman who had written a formal letter to the studio owner, requesting that he be allowed to take her home after a party. I asked him why taking her home would present such a problem; he laughed and said taking her home was a euphemism for something more.

When I asked students at the Tallahassee Arthur Murray studio to reflect on the challenge of maintaining friendships and professional relationships in spite of the intimacy of continually working together and possible attractions, hardly surprisingly, the married couples had no problems with maintaining that border, while singles admitted to having to work harder at it. Sarah Hurst, a divorcee, formerly married to a nondancer, replied candidly, "This is a tough one. It is very easy to let emotions get a free rein when you are working hard in an intimate posture with full body contact. . . . Keeping conversations on a light and jovial level is my best means of maintaining a friendly yet professional relationship. . . . Although sometimes when one of those little moments of ecstasy occurs, it's hard not to fall in love with your partner for a minute."[31]

The issue of harnessing one's emotions to appropriately express them within a context of professionalism brings up the related issues of whether one needs to feel something for the person one is dancing with in order to dance well, and whether acting out a role or simulating a virtual emotion in order to interpret the mood of the dance is necessary. The majority of the respondents replied that one needed genuinely to feel something but each interpreted what that feeling was differently. Fred and Anna Roberson replied that respect was the most important but that it was a big bonus when "your partner has a feel—and a flair—for the music—its dynamics, its rhythm, its mood. It is less enjoyable to dance with a wooden or milk toast partner."[32] Pat Erdman replied that what was most important for her was that her partner remain "thoughtful, tactful, never hurt[ful of] my feelings."[33] Sarah Hurst spoke of feeling "comfortable as a prerequisite to not dancing stiffly," Ann Mock, of the need to like someone, and Ron Hock, of "feel[ing] the music and the excitement and enjoyment of your partner" as an imperative to dancing well.[34] Only Eloise Harbeson, a gold-level dancer who is a veteran at competitions (and thus the art and sport of competitive performance) replied, "You need to have confidence in the partner's ability. If you mean 'feel something' to be like a sexual feeling, it is not necessary. One may need to give the appearance of a relationship in competitions and exhibitions."[35]

Ballroom studio culture is a highly stable one. Every month, a schedule of group classes, ranging from beginners, to bronze level, to silver and gold levels, is announced. The dances range from the smooth dances (foxtrot, waltz, tango, Viennese waltz), to rhythm dances (rumba, chacha, mambo, samba, East Coast single and triple time swing, merengue), to country dances (polka, country waltz, two-step, West Coast swing), to more unusual repertoires, like the Argentine tango or the Lindy Hop, and occasionally, an international style of ballroom (as opposed to the American style), like the quickstep. The stability extends to the decorum of these classes: men are asked to line up on one side of the room, women on the other side. The leaders' (men's) parts are first broken down and demonstrated, and then the followers' (women's) steps are analyzed and shown. Then a couple demonstrate the steps in tandem, where either two teachers dance, or a student is selected to perform the step with the instructor teaching the class. Men and women pair up, trying the steps in keeping with the instructor's counting, first without music, then with music. Rotation occurs, ideally, with military precision, with women moving in a clockwise motion to the next men, who stay stable—the anchors who maintain the order of who is supposed to dance with whom next. The goals of these group classes include the practice of well-known patterns for the more experienced dancers and the introduction of new patterns for both veterans and newcomers alike, for possible further refinement in private lessons with studio teachers.

Private lessons, which are scheduled in consultation between student and teacher, occur depending on which package the student purchases; in general, meetings range from as many as two or three times a week to once in about a fortnight. Private lessons or coaching lessons are really what are expensive about doing ballroom (usually costing between about $80 and $125 for forty-five minutes), but it is usually through such lessons that one improves dramatically in technique and develops competitive routines. Every week as well, usually during Friday evenings, the studio sponsors practice parties, and students get a chance not only to practice as many dances as they would like, but to dance with as varied a number of partners as they can find. The ratio of women to men is usually not quite equal (roughly about two or three women for every man), but men and teachers (who function as male, whether they happen to be men or women), out of courtesy, attempt to rotate partners, though some couples choose to dance only with each other. After a certain number of lessons, students test out of a certain level by showing that they know both the names (or figure titles) of a sequence of steps and the steps theselves by demonstrating them in front of an instructor who is not their teacher. Just like any ordered school curriculum, the ideal is to advance from one level to the next (beginner, associate bronze, full bronze, associate silver, full silver, gold star, gold bar) in an orderly and thorough manner.

When I asked the students to talk about why they continued dancing, their answers were similar. Sarah Hurst replied that her motivations

included "exercise, social contact, and mental health."[36] Ann Mock spoke
of an "addiction" to the enjoyment of dancing, which Fred and Anna
Roberson seconded, speaking of themselves as "hooked."[37] Patricia Erdman
replied that her primary doctor always asks whether she is still dancing
because this keeps her happy and healthy, and Ron Hock spoke of the
"challenge to improve" as one of his primary motivations.[38] Yet the reason
for this enjoyment remained vague until I posed the question of what they
found to be the most rewarding and frustrating aspects of being part of the
studio system. It turned out that several pointed to the security that the
studio system enables. Eloise Harbeson spoke of the rewards that "dancing
with excellent dancers . . . and wonderful friends . . . in a safe environment" presented.[39] Leonard Elzie added, "It's a good atmosphere because
everyone is always upbeat and supportive. Most frustrating—cost of lessons
limits how much I take. Other frustration is that I can't remember the
figures after the class is over—but that is me."[40] Sarah Hurst echoed a few
of Leonard's insights: "The most rewarding are the quality of the instructors and the consistency of the music and surroundings. The most frustrating aspect is the requirement to complete a certain number of private lessons
in order to advance through the levels of competence."[41] Irene Padavic was
the only one to actively critique the economic structure behind the lessons,
revealing that most clientele prefer not to see these "natural"-seeming sub-
structures that she addresses head on: "The most rewarding for me is having
such competent instructors. I care a great deal about technique and feel that
I learn a huge amount in each lesson. I don't like being pressured to increase
my participation into the realm of showcases and competitions, however. I
realize that the instructor/student interaction is a market-based relationship,
but I have indicated the services I'm willing to purchase and not purchase,
and resent attempts to sell me on more."[42]

There is something about the studio that creates an insulated and
secure environment. All men are implicitly expected to treat all women
with gallantry and courtesy and to lead with gentleness and firmness, thus
keeping at bay the ever-lurking cultural presumption that men who dance
are not masculine enough. All women, regardless of their age, physical
appearance, or weight, fulfill, during that brief moment of communion
through dancing, their fantasies of beauty and grace. A young-looking and
slim grandmother in her fifties once confided that she thought the reason
why so many women like ballroom dancing is because pairs dancing allows
one to come close to being "hugged" while dancing. Unlike Latin club
dancing, where a man can often take dancing the merengue as a license
to slap his pelvic area close to a woman whose name he does not even
know, or swing dancing, where a man can presumptively think dancing
swing well means manhandling women into doing stunts (a potential peril

I often faced as a five-foot-one-inch tall woman of slight stature), studio dancing provides a safe space, both in terms of etiquette and the physical expenditure of energy.

Yet another draw to the studio appears to be an element of prestige. Studio dancing is associated with discipline and technique; in comparison, "street" or "club" dancing is associated with spontaneity of expression and movement (along with smoke and alcohol). The outspoken David Mock replied with his blunt wit, "Ballroom is unique because it is orderly, mannered, refined. An illiterate and uncoordinated ape can do club dancing."[43] As I dance in several circles, once again, my insider-outsider perspective is instructive. At the Tallahassee American Legion Monday night dances, the crowd is highly varied in more ways than one: college students who belong to the Florida State University ballroom club come, as do ballroom aficionados of various types, whether studio trained or trained by independents, and country western dancers. Although there is a bar, unlike all-night clubs, no one shows any discernible signs of inebriation or does uncouth things like fling ice water or alcohol on the dance floor while laughing hysterically. College students usually dominate the floor during fast-paced swings, experimenting with lifts and stunts. Country western dancers enthusiastically take the floor with their acrobatic multiple turns when West Coast swings or two-steps are played. When music that can be interpreted in different ways, such as a waltz or a cha-cha, is played, numerous styles are showcased, ranging from the ballroom style, with its big top and elegant, long lines for the waltz, or its sensual Latin hip motion, for the cha-cha; or the country style, with its agile footwork and quick turns.

Yet despite the coexistence of different styles on the dance floor, one finds very few people who can move across the different communities. It is not simply an age difference, or the fact that people run in different social circles; neither is it simply not knowing enough common steps, though that is part of it. It is also the fact that different dances have different body languages, and translating across these bodily vocabularies is extremely difficult, and at times, unsettling. Ballroom dancers, particularly studio-trained ones, lead, oftentimes, from the chest or upper body, and often dance in closed position (that is, with the abdomen and hips in contact); those trained in a different tradition tend to lead from the hands and legs. These differences in styles of leading often render the points of communication between bodies incommensurable. Studio-trained dancers who advance beyond the basic level are trained to pay attention to the subtlest nuances—for example, whether it is a toe or heel lead; where the head has to be angled; how one styles one's hands. Dancers trained in a different tradition tend to be more concerned with moving to music in a rhythmical sense, maximizing their enjoyment of the movement in conjunction with the music. Country western dancers often use what seem to ballroom dancers like a dizzying number of turns, and swing dancers often incorporate aerials that ballroom dancers find dangerous, particularly when dancing with someone whom they do not particularly trust. Whenever I dance with someone who comes from a different dance tradition, whether male or female, it is of utmost importance to me that I remain sensitive to that person's level of comfort. Often, I half-jokingly beg the men to be gentle, particularly if they have a penchant for leading multiple turns; if they seem intimidated and constantly apologize for making a mistake while leading, I engage in lighthearted conversation. With a woman, I tend to lead simply the basics first and progress upward only if I sense that she is comfortable and confident. With other competitive female dancers, I attempt to lead more complicated and obscure moves, such as the *maxixe* in Samba, or several variations of the foxtrot twinkle, or the Tango *la puerta*. Moving across the leaders' and followers' parts, in addition to knowing formal patterns, and being flung into occasions where I have only my instincts to fall back on makes me appreciate the different skills that effectively leading and following necessitate.

I know that some women are uncomfortable with dancing with other women in social settings, and if I am aware that that is a problem, I simply do not ask them. But if men are not comfortable with a woman leading another woman perfectly willing to dance with a woman, there is nothing I can do about that. One of my tall female friends once whispered to me as we poised our bodies to begin a tango while we danced at the American Legion, "Do you know how many rednecks around here are uncomfortable with two women dancing together?" This was the first time I had heard of this, and I could only return a shocked look. "Ah," she said, throwing her nose humorously in the air with the exaggerated flair characteristic of the international style of the tango, "but we are secure enough in our femininities not to worry." And off we went. A few more dances down the line, a man invited me to dance with the words, "You do dance with men, too, right?" I grinned and accepted. Yet another young man, who was also a former trainee at the Arthur Murray studio, playfully remarked as he led me to the dance floor, "This time, you'll follow for a change."

I joined the Tallahassee Arthur Murray studio as a trainee in August 2000. What principally attracted me to the training program was the potential for improving my dancing and advancing through the levels at a faster rate than a regular student program would. I had already been teaching ballroom informally for a number of years: as an advisor to the University of Wisconsin-Eau Claire Ballroom Club, as a coteacher and demonstrator at a small studio at Eau Claire, as a dance consultant for several student groups at St. Lawrence University, and as an instructor of ballroom at the State University of New York in Potsdam. The instructors at the Arthur Murray studios at Eau Claire and Ottawa half-jokingly called me their "ex-officio" instructor because I often ended up leading at parties and group classes because of an imbalance in the gender ratio, and because new students tended to ask me to teach them a few very basic steps, which I willingly did.

I found, though, that being part of the studio system as a trainee (that is, a volunteer under training without pay, a choice I made as I did not want to jeopardize my duties as a university professor) changed a number of things. Particularly as a trainee (once again, another insider-outsider position: not quite a paid instructor, not quite a student), earning no money, but spending a lot of time at the studio, assisting with demonstrations and basic classes, there were a lot more demands on my time and energy. There was also the requirement of fitting into the cultural milieu of the studio, which I found very different, particularly from the Ottawa studio—the Tallahassee studio is a much more relaxed and social atmosphere, and so there is a greater stress on "goofing off" and having fun. Unlike the Ottawa studio, which often had elegant themes for its festivals, the Tallahassee studio, as its first theme party when I became part of its staff, had an "inside-out, outside-in" motif. I came wearing a shirt turned inside out, but was amazed to find the rest of the staff had gone well over the required limit: underwear worn over jeans; panties slung over heads like hats; teeth colored to resemble decaying cavities. I knew then that I had entered a different cultural milieu.

I sometimes felt that the analogy to being on call was an accurate depiction of the arrangement as a trainee. As someone at the bottom of the proverbial totem pole, I had to make myself as available as possible or run the risk that someone else could get assigned; at any time, an appointment with a potential student could be scheduled or cancelled. I found that the most important skills to being an instructor, particularly at the beginning level, were more business oriented rather than dance oriented. Even though one might be tired or stressed or discouraged, one had to force oneself to be supremely cheerful, perky, and outgoing, joking with students, or being attentive to their every need or anxiety. The usual ritual involved giving the studio tour and then beginning the basics of the general package, which usually included the foxtrot, waltz, rumba, and swing, although occasional deviations, if the student was particularly interested only in Latin dances, were allowed. We had a basic vocabulary to employ in teaching steps, including walking steps (whether forward or back), side (or "excuse me") steps, box steps (a composite of the walking and side steps in the figure of a box), rocking steps (shifting weight alternately from a front foot to a foot placed behind), and triple steps (tiny, shuffling steps done in triples, quick time). Thus, the basic of the foxtrot involved (for the man) two forward walking steps, executed as two "slows," and two "excuse-me" steps to the left, done in quick time. The waltz involved two half boxes, done to three-quarter time. The rumba, also composed of two half boxes, was taught to a slow-quick-quick time. The triple swing involved a rock step and two triple steps. The triple steps were often the hardest to teach because they involved quick, coordinated movement, in time to a fairly fast beat, which not everyone could do quickly. If a student was having difficulty with a triple step, then we were instructed to shift to a "single" swing, substituting a simple weight change for a triple step, thus preventing the peril of frustrating the student.

When I attended a training seminar in Atlanta in October 2000, I was struck by the rhetoric employed to discuss the business and art of teaching ballroom. One of the lecturers gave a long talk on the differences between a university professor (who, in his caricature, disinterestedly went on and on without audience contact) and a ballroom instructor (who, in his model, was perfectly attuned to every single need his students had—both in terms of dance and emotional and psychoanalytic terms). It became clear to me that the main distinction (in terms of institutional arrangements and cultural characterizations) is that whereas university professors have the "leisure" of teaching required classes, and society in general values education as a means to a practical end, ballroom instructors have to cultivate a *need* for continuing to dance, and ballroom lessons are considered a luxury, rather than a necessity to being successful in one's chosen professional career. Thus, the burden of proving that ballroom classes are essential and worth their price tags lies squarely upon the ballroom instructor's shoulders. Ballroom lessons within a franchised studio system easily cost thousands of dollars per package (though various payment schemes are allowable)—and this is not counting the cost of doing competitions, with their five-star hotel accommodations, custom-made costumes, jewelry and shoes, and preparatory coaching lessons. Ballroom is the heady stuff of dreams and fantasy, but it requires quite a financial lining to continue living the dream.

If one were to be an effective part of the franchise, one had to learn how to sell as many lessons as one could, and as effectively as possible. Though I greatly enjoyed the individualized coaching and group dance lessons that came with the seminar, perhaps a crucial factor that made me decide that teaching ballroom within the studio system was not for me was another short lecture on how to use touch to establish trust with one's students. I suddenly wondered whether my past teachers, with whom I thought I had established friendships, had thought of me as simply another number in the grand competitive push for earning the maximum number of lessons. When I discussed this matter with a friend and fellow teacher, Hope Cantrell, she replied candidly that though one could never neglect the business end of things, friendships, when they blossomed, were often genuine. Gaspar Van Der Ree, perhaps one of the gentlest human beings I have ever met, who was also a business manager at the Tallahassee studio, shrugged resignedly and said, "It is a business. One can never forget that."

When I asked ballroom instructors at the Tallahassee studio to reflect on what they found as the most rewarding, frustrating, and challenging aspects of teaching ballroom within the studio system, then-twenty-five-year-old Hope Cantrell, one of the veterans who had taught at the studio for three years, replied, "Very rewarding is the sense of camaraderie and belonging. Rather like a church group. Being part of a large franchised studio, like Arthur Murray, also affords us the opportunity to attend workshops and conventions, and have coaches visit. Frustrating are the rules. Any system has them, yet everyone has at least one that they don't see a need for."[44]

I was curious to find out whether teachers would respond differently from students in reflecting on the implicit gendered, racial, and class dynamics in ballroom, and was not too surprised to find a more homogenous response. Maurice Smith, a fifty-one-year-old US Coast Guard–licensed captain and then very new instructor at the studio, replied, "Over the centuries, the roles of men and women have varied, and probably will in the future."[45] Regarding race and class, he replied, "Now, race and class seem minimal."[46] Tillman Kasper, then a nineteen-year-old but already a senior teacher, saw any racial or class depictions in ballroom as "subjective" and no longer relevant.[47] Allison Drake, then a twenty-year-old trainee and part-time bartender, replied, "Honestly, I think it is nice; it is a bit old fashioned but it does work, and men do need one place they can be in charge."[48] Allison had an interesting anecdote to share regarding racial presuppositions and particularly Latin dancing: "My boyfriend is Latin, so his response when I ask him to take lessons with me is: 'I don't need to; it is in my blood.' "[49] In slight contrast, Hope Cantrell's reply wavered in between gender neutrality and a hint of biological and sociological determinism: "The lead/follow issue seems awfully sexist, but it doesn't bother me. . . . Someone had to lead and in most male/female cases, the female is better equipped to follow. I have only met a few men who could truly learn to follow. Whether it is socialization or something biological, it is something I have observed fairly consistently."[50]

Julie Taylor, in *Paper Tangos*, recalled some of her Argentine tango classes in which the "natural" gender arrangement was experimentally and temporarily loosened:

> We had thought we were close to something new when in a few classes the women had been told to lead the men. . . . What was interesting was the idea of the exchange of energy. If one dancer felt moved by the interaction or by the setting or by the music to launch a movement, she could smoothly take her partner into the embrace usually reserved for the man, and lead. . . . *But once we stopped, possibilities closed down. The instructor asked the men for their reactions and commented merely that now they would know the male role better.* A bit taken aback, one of the women, who had not been asked for her opinion, inquired, "And wouldn't this also offer a choreographic possibility?" No, the response came back. *This had only served to enhance the men's lead.*[51]

It is possible that this potential fluidity is unique to the Argentine tango, in which there are perhaps two basic patterns. One pattern is the "crusada" (where the woman ends up with her legs crossed and on tiptoe, with most of her weight concentrated on the front left foot—which allows the man to play with weight changes; the figure transitions into the next through "fans" {where the man shifts the woman's weight using his upper torso and arms, moving her as if she were a cape and causing her to fan her legs out alternately}, and leg flicks). The second figure is the "salida" (the "exit," which resembles a waltz box figure). The rest appears to rely on bodily communication and interpretation. Arthur Murray studios have an Argentine tango syllabus that has a stylized set of steps, but this differs sharply from the other types of tango training I have received, in which hours were literally spent simply walking backward or forward or shifting weight, with different partners, in order to gain the appropriate bodily vocabulary and sensitive attunement to give and receive directions.

As trainees, men and women were supposed to shift regularly from leader to follower positions, and within the context of practicing or training, this happened fairly frequently, though with pairs always remaining heterosexual. I never saw a male teacher experimenting with leading or following another male. Within the context of practice parties or group classes, the male instructors, who were often in great demand as leaders, remained in the leadership role, whereas females tended to cross gender lines more consistently, due to the imbalance in gender ratio. A former Arthur Murray instructor turned psychology professor at St. Lawrence University, Loraina Ghiraldi, divulged that in some studios, whenever the instructors see two women (particularly students) dancing, there is an imperative immediately to get them paired with men, and male instructors in particular are asked to cut in. Sometimes a male instructor, to fulfill competing duties, would dance half of the musical number with one woman and then apologetically excuse himself to dance with another woman.

The only times I have seen a woman actively and legitimately lead a male instructor in a studio setting is if the woman is a coach and needs a male partner in order to experiment with choreographic possibilities. Shirley Johnson, one of the most influential judges of the Arthur Murray circuit, and three-time undefeated Latin champion, often came to the Tallahassee studio for coaching sessions. It was very instructive to watch her shift fluidly and seamlessly from leader to follower roles, but even more interesting to watch her remain in the role of the feminine follower while obviously being the shaper of the movement. Male instructors good humoredly joked about this dominance, either simulating puppylike obedience or military compliance.

Regarding racial and class depictions, Hope's comments evaded the issue to some extent, but then arrived at a crucial insight: "I've never reflected on any race depictions. But one of the things I've always loved about dancing is that anyone can do it, and thanks to the play-acting part of it, any woman can be Cinderella for a while and any man can be in charge for a while."[52]

While I was listening to Hope, I realized that a large part of the power of fantasy in ballroom lies in its ability to obliterate, or at least render invisible, such categories as race and class and to render traditional heterosexual gender distinctions, in some ways, as not only inevitable but also highly desirable. Both the rhetoric and the practice of studio life demand this in order for the magic of ballroom to work. To begin to destabilize those categories is to deform the aesthetic, and with that, its boundaries of comfort and familiarity. Speaking as someone who continues to study ballroom, this insight does not necessarily detract from the beauty, enjoyment, and power of ballroom dance, but it does give me reason to pause when I reflect on how the genealogy of a dance usually differs radically from its professionalized, competitive form. For example, the tango, originally a dance of the bordellos, a dance mourning faithless love, a dance born in intense poverty and unhappiness, through the alchemy of choreographed ballroom dance becomes a glamorous, dramatic dance, often dissociated from its less genteel roots. Yet it is this polished look that becomes classified as more authentic looking somehow in the realm of professional ballroom dance, as well as in the public eye, which now avidly consumes public television broadcasts of DanceSport competitions.

AN OVERALL SCHEMA

The architecture of this book is as follows. Chapter 1, "The Contested Landscape of Ballroom Dance: Culture, Gender, Race, Class, and Nationality in Performance" is principally an explanation of the scope of the book and the various methodologies it employs. A subsection of this chapter, "Watcher and Watched: Insideness and Outsideness in Living, Writing, and Theorizing the Ballroom Dancer's Body," examines the rich continuum of social and studio dancing, using field notes and interviews with participant-performers. A crucial dimension of the approach I use is grounded in my own experiences, not only as racially hybridized, but also drawing from different dance traditions and communities. This, together with Chapter 2, establishes my point of entry into the topic as an insider-outsider or practitioner-critic of ballroom. Chapter 2, "Dancing through Different Worlds: An Autoethnography of the Interactive Body and Virtual Emotions in Ballroom Dance," employs autobiographical, phenomenological and autoethnographic methods in describing and analyzing the dynamics of competing in ballroom within a franchise studio format. Chapter 3, "Ballroom and the Movies," examines the complex cinematic heritage of continuity and disruption between Astaire-Rogers musicals and contemporary films that use a ballroom or DanceSport motif, and as such disseminate DanceSport's glamour in popular culture, and informally strengthens its bid for the Olympics. Chapters 1–3 describe the vast array of cultural landscapes within which the debates on whether ballroom dance should be packaged as an art rather than a sport are rooted using a variety of approaches. Chapter 4, "Paving the Road to the Olympics: Staging and Financing the Olympic Dream," covers the rhetorical arguments mounted by advocates and detractors of the proposal to transform ballroom into its Olympic competitive version, DanceSport. Such rhetorical arguments are ultimately tied up with material economic and business-related structures and considerations. Since this chapter references a great variety of dance-related organizations, a list of these groups, together with their contact information and websites, when these are available, are provided at the end of the book. Chapter 5, "Packaging Fantasy and Morality," focuses on depictions of gender, sexuality, race, class, and nationality in DanceSport and examines the aesthetic, political, and rhetorical dimensions of staging ballroom as an international competitive sport. Chapter 6, "Quo Vadis?," includes new directions that could be further explored, such as choreographic experiments in showdance competitions, films, and stage productions. The appendix is a selected filmography of movies that use the ballroom or DanceSport motif from the 1980s onward as earlier periods have been covered by other scholars. Finally, this book also includes photographs by Carson Zullinger and Cecil Greek.

TWO

Dancing through Different Worlds

An Autoethnography of the Interactive Body and Virtual Emotions in Ballroom Dance

The following is a reflection on my own experiences of the nature of gendered and embodied interaction in the realm of competitive American-style ballroom dance, which is presented predominantly in the form of a video, funded through research grants from St. Lawrence University. Issues of femininity/masculinity, being subject-objects of the aesthetic gaze, and issues of freedom and constraint are paramount to the exploration of what it means to do ballroom as both a competitive event and an art form. Normally, when I do a performance version of this chapter, after showing clips from the video that highlight interaction (for example, the nature of the gaze, leading and following, feminine and masculine bodies in smooth and rhythm dances), I incorporate live demonstrations of relevant steps and positions that highlight the points made regarding the relational and constructed nature of these virtual gestures. For this written format, I am substituting the incorporation of still photographs, grabbed from video footage, in order to help visualize the flow of the piece.

One of the aims of this chapter is to use frame grabs from the video in order to highlight the experience and expression of virtual emotions, such as passion, flirtation, attraction or repulsion, trust, and haughtiness in American-style ballroom smooth dances (such as the foxtrot, waltz, and tango) and American-style rhythm dances (such as the cha-cha, swing, rumba, mambo, and samba) (see fig. 2.1). The expression of virtual emotions (using Langer's[1] view that an essential characteristic of art is not literality but artifactuality, however genuine and spontaneous it may appear) is intimately intertwined with other issues, such as the nature of the aesthetic

Fig. 2.1   Posing to begin: feeling the relentless weightlessness of gazes. *(Photo courtesy of Cecil Greek)*

gaze, the gendered politics of leading and following, and the construction of feminine and masculine bodies.

"Heat number 19. Swing Routine. Silver level. Caroline Picart."

"Heat number 95. Cha-cha routine. Silver level. Caroline Picart."

With the announcer's voice trailing off into applause, my ballroom teacher, Mike, leads me to the floor, locating us in an area in which we best harness both the judges' and audience's gazes. The moments of stillness prior to the music beginning are perhaps the most challenging, as I become aware of the relentless weightlessness of gazes that inadvertently impale. My body and mind, taut with anticipatory tension, find catharsis as the music begins, and my partner initiates the playfully sensual movements of the cha-cha. For what seem like long moments suspended even as they flow, I allow the carefully choreographed movements of the dance, undulating with the rhythm and mood of *Tres Deseos*'s segmented fluidity and light, flirtatious sensualism, as initiated by my partner, to dance themselves out, using my body, in conjunction with his, as the canvas upon which gesture, mood, and emotion manifest themselves.

To me, dance is an art form that draws its breath from the volatility and transitoriness of its character as an animate composition in space and time, underlining and defying that spatiality and temporality. As Martha Graham writes, "A dancer's art is lived while he is dancing. Nothing is left of his art except the pictures and the memories when his dancing days are over. What he has to contribute to the sum total of human experience must be done through the dance. It cannot be transmitted at any other time, in any other way."[2]

Sally Peters points out, "Ballroom not only constitutes a singular landscape, but also the constantly emerging forms of dance establish their own landscapes of desire. Thus, the landscape of the waltz is all elegance, the fox trot all sophistication. The rumba is balletic seduction while the cha-cha, a triple mambo that is cousin to 'Dirty Dancing,' is high spirited and playfully sensual, while the swing, part fox trot, part jitterbug, is zippy and brash. In each dance landscape, my body assumes a characteristic and different look, so that individual dances can be identified from a still photograph. . . ."[3]

Having been trained in ballet for sixteen years, and for a less extended period of time in Hawaiian and Philippine folk dance, I am constantly reminded of how different dances imprint different bodily memories, leaving habits that are virtues in one and weaknesses in another. In ballroom smooth dances, where the upper body is stressed, the elegance and regal bearing and graceful lightness of the arms that years of ballet training ingrains are an asset (see fig. 2.2).

The use of long skirts with delicate, gauzy materials, often in pastels, helps generate the illusion of weightlessness and mystery; along with the elongated necks and accentuated backs, the pull of the smooth dances, in particular the waltz and the foxtrot, is upward. Interestingly, though ballet, too, strives toward a seemingly effortless suspension and defiance of gravity, its toe leads and foot turnouts, often acquired after countless exercises at the barre, become impediments to overcome in ballroom smooth dances. One of the most challenging bodily memories I have worked hard to instill is that of always aligning my toes with my heels in straight lines as I stretch back or forward, rising and falling through the combined action of knees and heels, moving, when necessary, between heel and toe leads (see fig. 2.3).

The tango is nominally a smooth dance by virtue of its closed position; temperamentally, it differs radically from the delicate weightlessness of the waltz and the polished sophistication of the foxtrot. Formally, the dance requires bent knees and an exaggeratedly arched back, generating a tense, erotic energy like that of a sleek wildcat ready to pounce. The sculpting of the body is in keeping with the temperament of the dance, which is steeped in a fierce eroticism and a haughty attraction/repulsion, whose shadowy origins lie in the bordellos of Argentina (see fig. 2.4).

Fig. 2.2 In ballroom smooth dances, the upper body is stressed. *(Photo courtesy of Cecil Greek)*

Fig. 2.3 Along with the elongated necks and accentuated backs, the pull of the smooth dances is upward. *(Photo courtesy of Cecil Greek)*

Fig. 2.4 The tango requires bent knees and an exaggeratedly arched back, generating a tense, erotic energy. *(Photo courtesy of Cecil Greek)*

The rhythm dances, in contrast, push the body earthward, overtly combining, to varying extents and in different modes, erotic sensualism with glamour. The toe leads and turnouts that I work hard to suppress in the smooth dances become crucial to good technique in the rhythm dances, such as the rumba, the cha-cha, and the mambo. All these require Latin motion, in which my legs are alternately bent and straight, as my pelvis subtly and sinuously thrusts backward and forward, with my body weight forward and my hips thrust backward, creating a distinctive line. Were it not for the fact that the movements are designed to flow into each other, I would appear to be segmented into upper body, waist, hips, knees, and the balls of my feet.

The rumba, "the dance of love," combines graceful sensuality with dramatic spiral turns. As the slowest of the rhythm dances, it is extremely unforgiving in its exaction of precision of technique as well as intensity of evocation.

The mambo is energetic and exudes erotic energy, building from a three-step heel/ball change danced to four beats, in which the first beat is a pause—which is perhaps the most tricky feature of this dance.

The cha-cha, a triple mambo, is flirtatious and light, requiring staccato movement.

The quintessentially American of the rhythm dances, the East Coast swing, combines the vigor and athleticism of African-American-inspired movements with elements of European partner dancing (see fig. 2.5).

The hustle, derived from the swing, incorporates disco elements with a smoother, more angular look.

The merengue is playful and fast paced, requiring mastery of Latin motion executed in beats of two and in basic figures of eight counts.

Interestingly, the general differences between the American-style smooth and rhythm dances may be seen as analogous to the differences between classical ballet and modern dance described by Sondra Horton Fraleigh: "The grace of ballet is not primarily of the earth but of spirit and air. The grace of modern dance is born of the sensuous, life-renewing serpent spiral." An even rougher analogy could be the stylistic similarities and differences between Ruth St. Denise's sensual etherealism and the raw, erotic sensuality of Martha Graham—whom Ted Shawn (Graham's teacher and husband of St. Denise) once described as a "beautiful . . . untamed . . . black panther."[4]

Fig. 2.5 The East Coast swing combines the vigor and athleticism of African-American-inspired movements with elements of European partner dancing. *(Photo courtesy of Cecil Greek)*

Nevertheless, one distinctive trait of ballroom dancing is its dependence on blending two bodies into one, particularly in the closed position. Though the man leads, often from the diaphragm and shoulders, and in some moves, such as in the tango, from the pelvis and thighs, it is not a crude imposition of power: when he moves his body against hers, she, in seamless fluidity, acquiesces, both to his lead and the power of the music enveloping them. Nevertheless, she is never an unthinking puppet: her responsiveness—which requires that she combine decisiveness (particularly in her forward steps) with nonanticipation, an almost oxymoronic combination of aggressiveness with infinite pliability—is crucial to generating the dynamic that constitutes their identity as a dance couple (see fig. 2.6).

Occasionally, I, too, lead, and it is fascinating to move from a position of alertly waiting to subtly initiating. The capital crime of following is anticipating a move; the unforgivable sin of leading is hesitating. Clear but gentle directives, mentally mapped before they are executed and communicated through the frame, are imperatives (see fig. 2.7).

When I change partners, I am thoroughly absorbed by the challenge and exhilaration of adjusting, discovering, and experimenting with the new parameters of bodily communication these occasions require. As Peters writes:

Fig. 2.6 One distinctive trait of ballroom dancing is its dependence on blending two bodies into one. *(Photo courtesy of Cecil Greek)*

Fig. 2.7 Occasionally, I, too, lead, and it is fascinating to move from a position of alertly waiting to subtly initiating. *(Photo courtesy of Cecil Greek)*

> The possibility of personally expressive movement adds an important aesthetic dimension for me and signifies the essence of ballroom dance—an expansion of self through another. . . . I feel the dance through my partner's body, and he through mine. The meaning of the dance is intimately and inseparably bound into our pairing, even as it enhances our private perceptions of self, perceptions expressed through movement that is stylized into what our culture defines as "feminine" or "masculine." . . . Once my body is accustomed to my partner's body, however he may move, whether or not I am familiar with the pattern, somehow my body "knows" its part."[5]

Yet part of the beauty and the power of ballroom dance, as an art form, lies in its ability to span the differences between thought and feeling, the actual and the imagined, reality and artifice into a complex continuum. Long hours of repetition, the strain of mental and emotional discipline, conscientious attention to detail, the unseen frenzy of changing into and out of costumes at fairly lightning speed—all are rendered invisible in this magical world of masquerade and mirage, resulting in what Laban calls a "feeling-thought-motion,"[6] which is paradoxically spontaneous and rehearsed, felt and imagined, real and virtual, self-expression and self-transcendence.

As Susanne Langer writes:

> In the dance, the actual and virtual aspects of gesture are mini-
> mized in complex ways. The movements, of course, are actual;
> they spring from an intention, and are in a sense actual gestures;
> but they are not the gestures they seem to be, because they seem
> to spring from feeling, as indeed they do not. . . . The emotion in
> which such gesture begins is virtual, a dance element, that turns
> the whole movement into dance-gesture. But what controls the
> performance of the actual movement? An actual body-feeling,
> akin to that which controls the production of tones in musical
> performance—the final articulation of *imagined* feeling in its ap-
> propriate physical form.[7]

As I am gallantly escorted off the floor, my arm tucked into Mike's
ever-gentlemanly arm, I reflect on how the allure, joy, and challenge of
ballroom dance remain perhaps impenetrable to outsider eyes. There will
always be the spectacle, the glamour, the mirages, the competitive rush, the
applause, and the awards. But beyond these, for me, is an unadorned confrontation with one's bodily, emotional and spiritual limits in dynamic conversation with a partner, music, and a larger audience—a testing of whether one
can, for a brief moment in time, surrender oneself to the unfolding of the
richness and vastness of being mere human flesh that for an all too brief
period, may become an embodiment of something that transcends mortality.

Ultimately, this chapter intersects with an interdisciplinary focus on the
body as an instrument of research and the performance of emotional labor
in several ways. With a few exceptions, such as Gurevitch,[8] though much
has been written on key concepts of embodiment, identity, and representation, dance (and in particular ballroom dance), for the most part, has
remained undertheorized. Indeed, many of the most influential investiga-
tions of the body have focused on two- and three-dimensional visual
representation (for example, film and the visual arts), where the material
and emotional dimensions of dance become submerged. Yet as Ness writes,
"[There is] a kind of meaning different from what most historians, political
scientists, economists, and other social scientists have studied and valued,
for it is meaning that develops in relation to essentially creative or *origina-
tive* figures of thought and action. It is meaning that must emerge from
personal and subjective reflection, and in an attuning to the moment-to-
moment experience of being physically alive."[9] It is precisely from such a

location that my autoethnographic voice roots itself. My experimentation with exploring the material, phenomenological, subjective, and interactive aspects of ballroom dance as an aesthetic, social, and competitive performance has been what I have sought to sketch, with the aim of inviting readers to "dwell within."[10]

Looking at dance requires that we begin to find a rich vocabulary for talking about dimensions like emotion, expressivity, sensation, and proprioception that do not fall prey to the Scylla and Charybdis of scientism and the construction of some transcendent, ahistorical and unified "self." Examining ballroom dance, particularly as a social and competitive event, necessitates that we theorize the complex relationships binding the public display of bodily movement and the articulation of social categories of identity and gendered bodies, as well as their transmission, transformation, perception, enactment, and communication. These complex negotiations are also what are at the heart of whether and how ballroom dance can effectively transform itself into an Olympic sport.

In chapter 1, I analyzed symbolic constructions of ballroom dance, as located across the cultures of the studio and the public dance hall. The approach taken in that chapter moved across the autoethnographic and the more conventionally ethnographic, building from interviews with social dancers, competitive dancers, neophyte and senior teachers, and coaches. In this chapter, I have relied upon a more phenomenological and autoethnographic approach in an attempt to explain why I continue to be drawn to the practice of ballroom despite my ambivalences as a critic, performer, and competitor. In the next chapter, the focus again moves outward, as I use tools of film criticism to analyze rhetorical constructions of gender, race, class, sexuality, and nationality implicit in cinematic depictions of ballroom dance.

THREE

Ballroom Dance and the Movies

INTRODUCTION

The transformation of ballroom into DanceSport to some extent is rooted in its popularity in contemporary films. There is a broad range of films that use a ballroom motif (see the appendix for a filmography of some of these). The ones that I focus on in this chapter are among the best known, and despite their multiple international origins (Japan, Australia, England), have achieved a popular following or public profile in the United States. All of these films clearly set themselves up as heirs to the Fred Astaire-Ginger Rogers-Gene Kelly musicals, yet they also attempt to locate these formulaic plots in more contemporary settings, thus setting up a visual rhetoric of nostalgia and realism. While they clearly exploit the glamour of the musicals of the 1930s and 1940s and often reify stereotypes of gender, race, class, and sexuality, they also allow for an ambivalent critique of these traditions. A common narrative thread running through these films is the notion that "genuine" dancing is tied up with not only self-expression, but also with a certain primitivism that resists conventional mores. Arguably, this convention may be traced to a common convention in Fred Astaire and Ginger Rogers films in which Fred croons of his primitive and salacious desires for Ginger under the most decorous and elegant of disguises—one of the most beloved examples of this is the "Night and Day" number in *The Gay Divorcee*. Here, Guy Holden (Fred Astaire) attempts to prevent Mimi Glossop (Ginger Rogers) from fleeing from him by beginning his fancy dance serenade with the lyrics, "Like the beat beat beat of the tom tom/ when the jungle shadows fall." This forms a continuity with the primitive passions characteristic of the "Carioca" number from *Flying Down to Rio*, the first movie that launched their dance partnership, even if they played supporting, rather than the main, roles.

The irony is that this "primitivism" ultimately turns out to be as glamorous and as formulaic as its supposedly staid counterpart. In addition, romanticizing the exotic (Cuba in *Dance with Me* and *Dirty Dancing: Havana*

Nights) becomes a way through which it becomes depoliticized. Racial and class differences, while they are addressed, are set up as temporary obstacles that will eventually be overcome—even if the glorious conclusion is simply one sensuous summer in which a girl becomes a woman, as in *Dirty Dancing* and its most recent remake, *Dirty Dancing: Havana Nights*. Nevertheless, ballroom films function in complex ways. They do not simply glorify the usual white, male, heterosexual, upper class-ideals: there are also clear ways in which these are problematized, as in Sally Potter's much maligned *The Tango Lesson*, in which a female directorial gaze is unabashedly voyeuristic. As such, these films function as sites for both tradition and transgression. Martha Nochimson makes the claim that despite their costuming, Astaire and Rogers enact their genders in a more androgynous than conventional mode. For example, regarding the "Cheek to Cheek" dance in *Top Hat*, Nochimson remarks: "The conventional grammar of masculine and feminine glamour implicated in the tuxedo and evening gown worn by Astaire and Rogers is complicated by the energies in the image. The rigidity of the white tie and black tuxedo . . . is contradicted by Astaire's flexible and light footed body. . . . Similarly, the pale evening gown worn by Rogers . . . yielding the stereotypically feminine aura of fragility and yielding, is at odds with Rogers's substantial, feminine self-possession, conveyed not only in her powerful body tone but also in the smooth and precisely coifed crown of golden braids in which her hair is dressed."[1] Since many of the more recent films that involve a ballroom or DanceSport motif style themselves as descendants of the Astaire-Rogers musicals, this gender blurring becomes even more pronounced in these films, while keeping them safely within a heterosexual erotic. Though many times this conflict falls back on a conventional resolution, it is not very easy to dispel the aftereffects of this transgression of boundaries.

DIRTY DANCING (1987) AND
DIRTY DANCING: HAVANA NIGHTS (2004)

Dirty Dancing's box office success in 1987 has been attributed to a number of factors: Patrick Swayze's crowning as a "sensitive hunk," Jennifer Grey's perfect casting as a girl on the verge of becoming a woman, the movie's difference from the rambunctious, expensive blockbusters that populated the cinemascape at that time, and its pop soundtrack mixing golden oldies with then-hip songs that flooded the radio stations. The story is set in summer 1963, before the Kennedy Assassination, at a lodge in the Catskills, where extremely rich families vacation and having only ten pairs of shoes for the three-week event is considered tragic.

On one hand, there is little to connect this film to Astaire-Rogers musicals: rather than being a lighthearted comedy about how a man over-comes the usual obstacles in his pursuit of the ever-elusive woman on the bumpy road to True Love, *Dirty Dancing* is more centrally a female coming-of-age film. A crucial difference between Fred Astaire and Gene Kelly films has been phrased by Arlene Croce: "But the Kelly film is no longer a dance film. It's a story film with dances, as distinguished from a dance film with a story."[2] Similarly, *Dirty Dancing* has darker, melodramatic elements (such as a botched and illegal abortion) and an overarching plot from which the dance sequences flow.

Nevertheless, it is through the enchantments of ballroom dancing and her involvement with the rebellious and seductive Johnny Castle (Patrick Swayze) that the sexual initiation and emergence into womanhood of Baby Houseman (Jennifer Grey) occurs. In this sense, it continues the Astaire-Rogers tradition of enshrining dance (in particular the Latin mambo) as the magical venue within which obstacles, in this case particularly class differences, are overcome. Yet the film performs a complex dance between enacting nostalgia and groundedness in reality: As Tom Matthews reports, "According to the filmmakers, 'Dirty Dancing' is based on a real period in American dance history. Between the era of ballroom dancing and the late '60's, when partners tended to dance several feet apart, there was a wave of dirty dancing that seduced teenagers and infuriated parents."[3]

Idealistic and brainy Baby, who intends to join the Peace Corps, arrives at the lodge together with her parents (Jerry Orbach and Kelly Bishop) and her more materialistic and superficial sister (Jane Brucker). Baby is immediately paired off with the hotel manager's obnoxious son, but she is quickly bored by him, as well as with the hotel's standard forms of entertainment, such as volleyball and aseptic versions of ballroom dance reconfigured as line dances in this family-oriented lodge. Instead, she falls for the apparently unreachable Johnny, who gives dancing lessons to elderly love-struck and lonely women at the camp. By day, he teaches the finer points of the elegant fox-trot; by night, he either engages in "private lessons" of a very different nature for additional tips, or in secret staff dance orgies. The film's title is derived from this clandestine activity. Shot in slow motion and in close-ups that fragment and fetishize the dancers' youthful and sexy bodies (a perspective we have access to via the slightly scandalized but intrigued Baby), it is characterized by a preponderance of seductive, pouty lips, arched backs for the women, and thrusting pelvises for the men. Despite and because of its lower-class origins (only the economically sub-ordinate hotel staff partake in it; neither management nor clientele are usually allowed entry), it is characterized as the "real" dancing because of its primitivism and freedom from conventions (a common theme with the more genteel Astaire-Rogers musicals).

It is clear that the usual gendered dynamics of the chase are reversed: the pursued is the older, sophisticated man; the pursuer is the younger, gauche teenager-turning-woman. It is Swayze's naked upper body that the camera likes to linger on repeatedly; Grey's body, even when she undresses in the back seat of the car and is soaked with water from practicing lifts in the lake to soften possible falls, remains inaccessible to the voyeuristic gaze. Unlike Fred Astaire's initial screen test in Hollywood, which resulted in the legendary desultory report, "Can't act. Can't sing. Balding. Can dance a little,"[4] Swayze's sexual charisma and dance presence are universally acclaimed, sometimes, ironically, to his detriment. Steve Rhodes reveals how Swayze (whose screen presence seems more palpable than his character, Johnny Castle) in this film occupies a space akin to that inhabited by Mary Russo's notion of the "female grotesque,"[5] both dangerous and endangered: "Patrick Swayze, who delivers a terrific performance . . . when his mouth is firmly shut, plays an enormously handsome dance instructor named Johnny Castle."[6] Swayze's attractiveness and gracefulness render him a sex symbol—that ambiguous category of both empowerment and disempowerment, particularly for a male.

Unlike the eternally glamorous Ginger Rogers—whose elegance is not marred by accidents, as in her dress being accidentally caught in a trunk and then ripped in *The Gay Divorcee*, or her temper and gifts for physical comedy in *Top Hat* and *Roberta*—Jennifer Grey is particularly appealing in her role precisely because she is Rogers's opposite. As Pete Croatta perceptively observes, "Grey doesn't drip with teen sensuality or flash a come hither stare. She giggles inappropriately, she curses herself for not getting dance steps right. By embodying every awkward young adult emotion about falling in love, she makes you want the romance to work."[7]

Class (as intertwined with Jewish clannishness) appears to be a big issue in the film. Though Johnny is allowed some access to the realm of privileged and perfumed female bodies, that access is sharply delimited: he is essentially a gigolo, even if he has a heart of gold, and suffers from an inferiority complex he hides under a façade of nonchalance: "The reason people treat me like I'm nothing is because I'm nothing," he laments in one of his more vulnerable moments with Baby. What authorizes him as a romantic partner for the innocent Baby is his gallantry. Johnny's longtime professional partner, Penny Johnson (Cynthia Rhodes), is impregnated by one of the hotel's waiters—the son of a rich man who is momentarily employed as a waiter in order to mingle with the daughters of the super-rich. This same character is an Ivy League aspirant who reads Ayn Rand's *The Fountainhead* for moral inspiration. Johnny does his best to support his dance partner, particularly when her illegal abortion is botched. Class, the movie preaches, is no indicator of morality: the poor are capable of nobility, as the rich are capable of treachery.

The main lines of the story are quickly and predictably sketched: with Penny bedridden, Johnny needs a partner quickly for a looming professional engagement. Baby ambivalently offers to take her place, and Johnny slowly comes to appreciate her efforts. Baby's father, thinking Johnny is the irresponsible father of Penny's aborted child, violently sets himself up against their romance, leading to Baby's surreptitious meetings with Johnny, alternating between dance practices and erotic encounters, which the movie makes clear are essentially interchangeable with each other. Nevertheless, the camera visually differentiates between the innocence of these encounters, shot predominantly in high-key lighting, and the seediness of Johnny's relationships with his clients, one of whom attempts to blackmail him into continuing their nocturnal activities when he resists. Steve Rhodes remarks "Especially worth noting is [Jeff Jur's] choice of Baby's feet as a focal point. Her pristine white tenny runners never get a speck of dirt on them. As Baby dances on her little toes in her snow-white shoes, her innocence is actuated in ways that a full profile could never accomplish. He also does a good job of framing the two stars when they cavort in a dance number on a log over a small stream."[8]

Their relationship and dance partnership deepen, and they perform the number successfully together. Unfortunately, this leads to the discovery of their hidden romance, and Johnny ends up losing his job. Nevertheless, in the climatic conclusion, Johnny returns to perform his "dirty dancing" mambo number with Baby. Baby's family, along with the rest of the hotel vacationers, are initially stunned into silence, and then gradually move into enthusiastic support. The film, despite its extravagant conclusion, ends uncertainly. It is not clear whether Baby and Johnny will stay together in the long term: their social and class differences, momentarily submerged, remain specters in the background.

Dirty Dancing: Havana Nights is an attempt to capitalize on the tremendous economic success and popularity of its predecessor while apparently recasting it to reflect America's ambivalent sociopolitical relationship with Cuba. Billed as a "reimagining" of the original version, the new version relocates the setting from the pre-Kennedy-assassination Catskills to pre-Fidel Castro Havana, circa 1958. The now hackneyed plot follows the same pattern: a young, sheltered, privileged woman matures as she becomes entranced by the earthy, sexy abandonment of Latin ballroom dance, Havana style; she also awakens to the economic disparities and political turbulences that underlie the tourist-friendly exterior of Batista's Cuba. Like Grey's Baby, Romola Garai's Katey is a class brain but socially klutzy (a June Cleaver type). When her father Bert (John Slattery) takes a well-paying job with Ford in Havana, she is uprooted from her St. Louis high school. Her dad's employer's son, James Phelps (Jonathan Jackson), like the hotel manager's son in the original movie, is interested in initiating Katey into his cliquish, hermetic country club life; yet Katey's eye is drawn to Javier Suarez (Diego Luna), a poolside waiter who accidentally spills the drink of another American woman, Eve. Eve's racist belittling of Javier leads Katey to apologize for the other woman, but Javier proudly refuses the apology. After chancing upon Javier sensually gyrating in a public square, Katey voyeuristically follows him into the hidden realm of dirty dancing. Javier later saves Katey from an unwanted sexual overture by James. Like Johnny Castle, Javier is unjustly punished for his gallantry: he is also fired. Katey, realizing the Javier's family relies solely upon his meager income as a waiter to survive, comes up with a proposal that serves two purposes: he will be her dance partner at a prestigious national dance competition, and thus aim to win the grand prize to subsidize his family (and also thus learn more slinky moves from this Cuban hottie).

Seeking to step into the shoes of a highly successful predecessor is always skewed toward failure because one is constantly compared with the original. It is hardly surprising that both Garai and Luna receive mixed reviews for their performances, with the inevitable comparisons to the originals. While Jennifer Grey pulled off a believable awkwardness, particularly in attempting to master the box step, the voluptuous, full-lipped Garai's transformation from *gringa* to *salsera* is not as dramatic. Thus critical disagreements arise: Laura Clifford thinks Garai "does a nice job as the fresh-faced American girl who has hitherto ignored boys for books without succumbing to Pollyana-ish behavior."[9] In contrast, Eleanor Ringel Gillespie scathingly writes, "Apparently cast for her creamy blonde looks and her ability to lift her leg high, Garai is abysmally stiff and not the least bit interesting as character or actor."[10]

To reduce Garai's performance to her physical appearance may be too harsh, but Ringel Gillespie brings up a crucial point. Garai's screen presence is very different from Grey's. Garai is a very tall, very white blonde who dwarfs Luna slightly; it is not surprising that it is she who initiates the idea of a dance partnership, and partially challenges and partially seduces him into it. When Javier initially protests against the idea of a dance partnership, saying he wasn't auditioning to win a contest when they first danced at the nightclub La Rosa Negra, Garai's retort, "Oh weren't you?" is a complex blend of aggressive challenge and coy flirtation. Grey, in contrast, is a tiny brunette who musters a lot of spunk in her determination to become a proper partner to Swayze; but Swayze's physical size and commanding presence would not have allowed Grey to believably pull off what Garai's character managed to. Though Garai can appear genuinely uncomfortable when her conservative character dons a form-fitting red dress, and she can also look somewhat awkward as she practices in front of a mirror dressed in a tied white shirt and capris (a clear homage to the dance-related struggles of Jennifer Grey's Baby), Garai remains comparatively composed throughout the film.

In like manner, Luna received mixed reviews. Eleanor Ringel Gillespie, who detested Garai's performance, remarked that Luna "has all the talent and charisma Garai lacks. He's even prettier than she is. But I'm not sure how good a dancer he is; he's shot in the kind of cut-away style that suggests he is not."[11] Part of the problem was that Patrick Swayze also makes an appearance in this movie—a cameo in which he steals the show. In the role of the hotel dance instructor, he instructs and encourages Garai to let go and confront the fear of allowing someone to touch her, not only physically, but also emotionally. His screen presence, even as a much older man (now in his fifties), reanimates memories of his immortalized celluloid self, and Luna suffers from the comparison, especially in terms of his dance abilities.

In addition, the difference in ages, a crucial factor in Baby's credible initiation from teenager to woman through Johnny Castle's tutelage, is also obscured. Garai appears older when juxtaposed with Luna's boyish looks, with the consequence that their romantic dancing has been described as more akin to the interaction of "good friends rather than star crossed lovers, even when they're steamily intertwined at Rosa Negra."[12] As Carla Meyer remarks, the new couple's screen chemistry is more "affectionate" than "sexual," and when they kiss, they are not "believable."[13] The whole issue of credibility haunts this remake. Though the movie is based on choreographer JoAnn Jansen's personal experiences as an American girl in prerevolution Cuba, it is clear that she romanticizes her memories. The official trailer to the movie lingers on medium shots of Garai, her blonde hair tied back neatly and her white skin glistening in the glare of the beach sun; she is described as someone whose life is totally circumscribed by rules. Juxtaposed are medium shots of Luna, whose dark, wind-ruffled hair and dark skin mark him as the noble savage (this time devoid of Astaire's elegant trappings) whose lifestyle is characterized as "total freedom." The film may have been designed in order to give it more historical depth and political complexity, but if so, the attempt backfires. The attempted docudrama ends up a fairy tale built around another simplistic binary dichotomy: "The tourist paradise of Batista's corrupt, crime-ridden Cuba is contrasted with the sweaty, hearty, sexy Coo-ba of Havana's working population, where revolution is brewing under the driving salsa beat of its nightclubs and the blonde child of privilege is improbably tolerated by the brothers of rebellion."[14] The film's climax, the grand proclamation of their dance partnership and amorous involvement at the dance contest to Garai's initially shocked and eventually wildly enthused family is undercut by the eruption of revolutionary violence led by Castro. Harvey Karten amusedly recalls an acid remark growled by a colleague after watching the film: "The Cuban Revolution existed only to interrupt the dancing."[15] While the remark may be too judgmental, it is significant to note that part of the reason why this remake was deemed less successful in general than its predecessor was that it attempted to freight itself with a heavy political subtext—an even more significant departure from the lighthearted romantic and comedic musicals rendered iconic by the ballroom dream team, Fred Astaire and Ginger Rogers. Nevertheless, this film renders explicit what was implicit in the original *Dirty Dancing*: this is a nostalgic story of a young woman's coming of age in an exotic land; there is neither immortality nor even the hint of mortal marriage at the end. Garai's all-American ultra whiteness, juxtaposed alongside Luna's exotic nonwhiteness, emphasizes the impossibility of this union: unlike Astaire and Rogers, who know they are made for each other, Garai and Luna know all they have is one brief summer.

STRICTLY BALLROOM (1992)

Baz Luhrmann's trend-setting *Strictly Ballroom* was adapted from a fifty-minute Australian stage play which was originally conceived as a student project at the National Institute for the Dramatic Arts (NIDA). It then proceeded to tour Australia with resounding success and garnered several awards at an international competition in Czechoslovakia. Because the Australian producers were unable to solicit funding from overseas distributors or financiers, they turned to their own devices for raising funds and ultimately were able to gain sufficient control of the material to make it "their way"—one of those cases in which the production history of the movie remarkably parallels the film diegesis.[16]

The film's ambivalent connection with 1930s- to 1950s-style ballroom musicals is immediately trumpeted through various reviews. Rita Kempley of the *Washington Post* praises the film for its ability to "both tweak and embrace the conventions of the genre—from the boot shaking of 'Dirty Dancing' to the Latin sizzle of 'Flying Down to Rio.' "[17] Evan Hunt of *The Web* exclaims: "If you're the kind of person who sighs wistfully at the end of SINGIN' IN THE RAIN because they don't make movies like that anymore, rejoice—because they have! . . . [It is] a parody of every musical cliché that amazingly also rejuvenates the genre and makes it fresh and alive again."[18] But it is Roger Ebert who comes up with the most memorable description of the film, with a keen eye on its playful hybridizing of genre conventions: "The movie, which crosses Astaire and Rogers with Mickey and Judy and adds a dash of Spinal Tap, is a comedy posing as a docudrama about competitive ballroom dancing in Australia."[19] Desson Howe puns cleverly, "Grabbing every backstage musical cliché by the lapels, it sends each one pirouetting, then sprawling hysterically across the floor. It's hard not to love this kind of tribute."[20]

The story line itself is a sort of ugly duckling meets *Flashdance*. Fame-obsessed veteran dancer Mrs. Hastings (Pat Thomson) is appalled to find that her son, Scott Hastings (Paul Mercurio)—a virtual dance god slated for immortality with his looks, charm, and status as heir-apparent to the title of being the next Pan Pacific Grand Prix Champion—resorts to wild new steps, abandoning the Dance Federation's rigid steps in favor of his own moves. His partner, Liz (Gia Carides), reluctantly follows his lead during the contest but then tearfully places all responsibility for her "sins" on her headstrong partner in the pseudodocumentary interview that appears to reconstruct the events. Angry and terrified at his dangerous longings for originality, Liz leaves him. With only a few weeks before the competition, Mrs. Hastings begins to hold auditions with various prospective partners, shot in parodic simulation of the fairy tale prince's search for the perfect bride, in which the prince finds fault with every single possible candidate. Surprisingly, the ugly duckling, Fran (Tara Morice), a beginner with barely two years of experience, and coded as impossibly klutzy and nerdy by virtue of those large spectacles that obscure her features, appeals to be given a chance at partnering with Scott. Scott is initially insulted but then slowly changes his mind when he realizes Fran shares his passion for unorthodox steps and actually invents some of her own in private.

The plot line is unfailingly formulaic in its tracing of conventional story lines with its fidelity to expectations underlining precisely its attempt both to reify and debunk not only the genre of the romantic musical (rendered iconic by the Astaire-Rogers team), but also the mythical prestige of the competitive DanceSport circuit. As Mark Leeper remarks, "Here also is a delightful satire of really bad over-ripe dramatic story-telling. It is all here: the boy with the dream, the girl from the wrong side of the tracks, the pushy mother, the conspiracy to fix the big dance competition, the dark secret from the past, and, of course, the climactic dance competition."[21]

Nevertheless, the gendered, classed, and racial dimensions of the narrative reveals some departure from the usual Astaire-Rogers narrative. The major Astaire-Rogers movies, such as *The Gay Divorcee, Top Hat,* and *Swing Time,* are famous for the dances in which Rogers repeatedly attempts to flee from Astaire, only to be detained, drawn back, and eventually won over by the eloquence and elegance of his declarations of love through dance. In this movie, it is clear that Scott is the eroticized object, and the camera seems to savor its intercutting of tight close ups that linger on his glistening, rippling body with its full-body coverage of his powerful movements as he dances secretly at the deserted studio. Max Hoffman practically drools over Mercurio's physical attributes and charisma: "With a young Tyrone Power's face on Marky Mark's body, Mercurio is a candidate for the decade's next 'poster boy' role."[22]

It is also clear that it is initially Fran who is doing the chasing. Dressed in an oversized shirt, unbecoming slacks, and unfashionable socks, she seems the utter negation of femininity. Yet as she continues to work with Scott, her transformation from ugly duckling to ingénue renders her increasingly more conventionally feminine. She trades in the glasses and the oversized nondescript clothing for flower-printed dresses that emphasize her slim figure and ponytails that show her face—which is not conventionally beautiful, but sufficiently charming for the transformation and their budding love affair—to become believable within the standard heterosexual frame. Though her skin is also white, we later find out that she is actually the daughter of Hispanic immigrants whose lower-class status is evident in the small family store they run in order to make ends meet. Fran's outspokenness and independence, as the story progresses, is both undercut and enabled by her status as the daughter of an overprotective Hispanic father (Antonio Vargas), who, it turns out, is an expert at the "authentic" Paso Doble. It is she who translates her grandmother's and her father's questions and instructions to the humbled Scott, who is now determined to learn from his new father figure, given that his real father, Doug (Barry Otto), seems an ineffectual wimp wrapped up in his own world, cowed by his overly ambitious wife. Yet as Fran grows in her abilities as Scott's proper partner, she also becomes increasingly silent and pliant—even to the extent of sacrificing her aspirations when it appears Tina Sparkle (Sonia Kruger-Tayler), a dance champion, is determined to have Scott as her partner.

The plot unwinds in keeping with the usual narrative conventions: thus commences that training-over-time sequence, in which the main characters sweatily tread on toes, bump clumsily into each other, and eventually begin to achieve success—not only mechanically, but also emotionally—particularly when Fran one time takes off her glasses (the standard device by which an "ugly" woman metamorphoses into a desirable one), and Scott encourages her to dance with him without her glasses. Naturally, Scott and Fran begin to fall in love with each other; and just as naturally, obstacles of various sorts have to be set up for the story to be engaging. Mrs. Hastings redoubles her efforts at ensuring what she views as the most foolproof way of making sure Scott wins: tearing him away from his confused infatuation with an amateur and the dangerous desire to imbue his dance steps with genuine feeling and self expression rather than formal perfection. Rico, Fran's father, in classic patriarchal fashion, demands to know Scott's intentions and then challenges the young man to a duel of dancing the *Paso Doble*. In the same way Fran magically transforms from ugly duckling to ingénue by taking off her glasses, Rico transforms from repressive father to dance guru by throwing off his outer garments to reveal a lithe body impressively dressed in a bullfighter's top, to commence a twirling, stamping routine with Flamenco elements that clearly emasculates Scott's more conventional and "feminized" interpretation of the *Paso Doble*, with its light, graceful turns, devoid of the *gravitas* and hyperenhanced masculinity of Rico's interpretation.

The impetus of the film hinges on the binary opposition it sets up between the world of ballroom competition dancing and dancing as grounded in genuine emotions and lived experience. This contrast is particularly set up in one scene where Scott and Fran dance a silent, romantic rumba, wrapped up in each other's arms and gazes in the privacy of the deserted backstage. As perfect counterpoint, Tina Sparkle and her retiring dance companion perform their version of a "fruit rumba" on the other side of the curtain, bathed in the glow of spotlights and romancing the audience and the media rather than each other.

Formally, the film could not be further away from its Astaire-Rogers predecessors. There is a myth that one of Astaire's innovations in filming dance was to shoot in a single unedited take so as to allow the dance to speak for itself, untrammeled by distracting camera tricks. While this is not true, Astaire, once he had sufficient box office power as a star to control how his dances were shot, did tend to simplify how his dances were filmed, opting for invisible editing that enabled the dance to flow seamlessly, rather than be interrupted by standard devices like reaction shots from spectators or extreme close-ups that dismembered the feet from the rest of the dancer's body. As John Mueller observes, "Astaire quickly got rid of cluttered camera perspectives. Three of the shots in the "Carioca" duet . . . [in *Flying Down to Rio*] are framed in the foreground by posed observers, and Sandrich shot part of the "Night and Day" duet [in *The Gay Divorcee*] through Venetian blinds and another part from under a table. . . . Such distracting effects were never to be seen again in Astaire's dances."[23] In contrast, Luhrmann's vividly colored and tensely energetic dance universe has an equally hyperactive camera. Ebert remarks disapprovingly, "Luhrmann, like many first-time directors, is intoxicated with the possibilities of the camera. He uses too many wide-angle shots, in which the characters look like blowfish mugging for the lens."[24] Yet if the predominant mode of the film is parodic, then the deliberate overuse of the medium close-up-talking-heads format alongside a rough handheld-camera feel in order to simulate and deconstruct the conventional realistic modes of documentary filmmaking is appropriate. Similarly, the use of devices like the dissolve, slow motion, and extreme close-up on the Spanish bullfighter top that Scott dons—an inheritance from Rico—in order to emphasize Scott's dramatic entrance into the climactic competition is justified insofar as ballroom competitions tend to be edited in a similar fashion to inject drama, tension, and action. The frenetic movements of the camera parallels the madness and mania of the denizens of this particular universe, whose thorough obsession with winning the competition reveals how autistic their worlds have become. Interestingly, Scott's attempt at rebellion and anarchy, with the introduction of new steps, is just as thoroughly obsessed with dance as those whose universe he seeks to shatter. And just as the myth of the "real" dancer is tied up with some glorified ideal of primitivism—a freedom from conventions—the story of Scott's rebellion is just as conventionally visualized, as is evidenced in the way the concluding dance sequence is shot, with its use of spotlights that emphasize the whiteness of the transformed Fran's skin and the alternation between full-body shots and close-ups, typical of the way ballroom television productions frame dances.

THE TANGO LESSON (1997) AND TANGO (1998)

Though both *The Tango Lesson* and *Tango* are about the brooding beauty and haunting spirituality of the tango, and are highly proximate in terms of their dates of release, the differences between the two films are striking. *The Tango Lesson*, ranging across the settings of Paris, London, and Buenos Aires, is shot predominantly in black and white, save for the sequences, shot in intense Technicolor, depicting Potter's fantasies concerning an abortive screenplay about a grotesquely legless fashion designer killing highly stylized fashion models. The use of black and white gives the film a look both arty and pseudodocumentary. Because Sally Potter plays a woman director with her own name, and because the other principal character, played by the great Argentine tango master, Pablo Veron, also essentially plays himself, the audience is left wondering whether the film is autobiographical or not.

In comparison with *Tango Lesson*'s subtle and elegant black and whiteness, Carlos Saura's *Tango*, an Argentinean-Spanish production, has been described as an "orgy of colors and images—an intense sensory experience."[25] Vittorio Storaro's cinematography has received universal acclaim. Shadows and projections are just as important as three-dimensional bodies in his work. Thus, silhouettes of dancers are framed by a glowing white background, with background colors shifting as eloquently as the myriad emotions that inhabit a tango, sometimes radiating an angry red and at other times shimmering with a cool blue. Though it is clear that the movie is shot from the point of view of an aging and partially disabled director (Mario Suarez, played by Miguel Ángel Solá), the lines between imagination, fantasy, and reality in his interior world and rehearsal, real life, and performance in the exterior world he controls are so porous that it is difficult to tell them apart. The resultant film is more surreal than it is docudrama, even if it, like Potter's *Tango Lesson*, uses the motif of the film within a film (which, in Saura's case, is compounded with the production of a stage play within a film, alongside the film-within-a-film motif).

The same confusion does not exist in Potter's *Tango Lesson*. Potter's movement into a creative mode is signaled either through sharp glimpses in full color (as when she writes her screenplay for a film preliminarily titled *Rage*) or auditorily, through the persistence of a haunting instrumental as she gazes upon Pablo Veron, particularly in the kitchen scene. Here, Veron, finding out that Potter has decided to discard *Rage* in favor of a movie about the tango, turns the act of preparing a salad for dinner into an elaborate tap dance number. Like Fred Astaire, he taps out a rhythm with his feet and hands, defies gravity, and juggles bowls and literally tosses salad as if these were props for a movie rehearsal. He puts himself on display for Potter's voyeuristic enjoyment. The persistence of a proactive rather than reactive female gaze of desire along with its problematization of conventional boundaries of gender and power, which is evident in the prior movies discussed, continues in this film. This is a motif that may be traced to Fred Astaire films, as in the "Night and Day" number in *The Gay Divorcee*, where Astaire makes use of an "odd shuffling or supplicating 'mating' dance phrase"[26] in order to win over the initially icy Ginger Rogers. In the same way that Fred Astaire is secure in his skills of seduction through dance, so is Pablo. There is one crucial difference, though: Astaire's tap numbers often give one the sense that his limbs simply start to move, as if possessed, magically induced to movement by a force greater than his will. Regarding Astaire's tap solo that commences after the song "I Won't Dance" in *Roberta*, Mueller remarks, "The tap solo that ensues is a virtuosic, crazy-legged affair—it is as if Astaire were setting out graphically to develop the song's suggestion that he has no conscious control of his feet. There is a lot of limb slinging, and, between furious tap flutters, he is constantly finding one leg wrapping itself around the other."[27] In contrast, Pablo's movements are clearly masterfully and consciously staged. In one section, he jumps lightly on to a mantelpiece, right in front of large mirrors, and dances with his mirror image, who smiles back at him and follows him seamlessly. This is in sharp contrast with Sally, of whose dance following skills Pablo is often cruelly critical. The persistence of the mirror motif in relation to Pablo's gravitation toward narcissism is clearly marked in the film; his artistic gifts are not only tied up with a spontaneous but carefully harnessed primitivism, but also with a self-

centeredness that teeters between reinforcing his masculinity and destabiliz-
ing and reducing him to a spoiled child in Sally's eyes. In a later scene, when
Pablo finds out he is to be one of a trio of male tango dancers to be featured
in Sally's embryonic movie, he walks over to perform an Astaire-like solo
whirlwind, bringing it smoothly to a halt in front of some floor-to-ceiling
mirrors. After domesticating a rebellious strand of hair, he blows himself a
kiss, demonstrating to all that it is he who is the star of the film—a fact the
other male tango dancers take with good humor.

The Tango Lesson is essentially an occasion for showcasing some of
Veron's amazing choreography, and a sentimental romance between a middle-
aged woman and younger man who find out, despite their power struggles
(they both like to lead—he as a dancer; she as a director) and differences,
that they are essentially soulmates. Though Sally is a resident of London
and Pablo is an expatriate Argentinean living in Paris, they both speak
French and English, and eventually learn that they share an affinity for
Judaism: "I suppose I'm an atheist but I feel like a Jew," she declares in
response to Pablo's question of whether she believes in God. Pablo responds, "I am a dancer . . . and a Jew." This discovery leads them to shed
silent but joyful tears. In the sequence that follows, as Veron escorts Potter
to the airport to meet with some Hollywood bigwigs regarding her idea
for Rage, the relational dynamic is set up. Using objects that are characteristic of airports, such as carts and conveyor belts, the couple enact a complicated dance of multiple breaks and reconciliations, with Pablo at one
point laying himself horizontally across the elevated section of the conveyor belt and opening his arms wide in abandonment, as if crucified, as
Sally bends down to kiss him. That pose does not last long, though: shortly
thereafter, he straightens and bounds lightly over the conveyor belt edge
and disappears from sight, and then suddenly pops up as if to declare
complete control of his appearances and disappearances.

The main outlines of the thin plot of The Tango Lesson may be
sketched briefly. The film begins as Potter confronts the blank page, with
the walls in her apartment as white as the empty sheet in front of her.
Through sudden bursts of vivid color, we glimpse her imagination at work:
we see three gloriously dressed fashion models, one of whom is gunned
down by a legless wheelchair-bound man. We find out later, in the satiric
scene in which Potter converses with Hollywood producers by a pool, that
the legless man is a designer who becomes envious of the media attention
on the fashion models. Sally is distracted by an indiscernible flaw in her
floor and calls in a repairman, who humorously proceeds to take her whole
floor apart. She escapes from the apartment and wanders into a tango
performance by Pablo and his then-partner, played by Carolina Iotti. From
the very start, it is clear who commands the gaze. From her point of view,

we initially see just a confused jumble of the tops of heads as she struggles to gain view of the stage. Then there is a close-up of her face as she leans forward, entranced, to watch the fascinating spectacle of highly controlled spasms of kicks and leaps. The camera work deviates from Fred Astaire's standard as it is marked by the insertion of reaction shots and close-ups of legs and faces—a style of shooting that remains constant throughout the film; nevertheless, it underlines what Sally, as audience and director, considers the focal points of viewing.

Entranced, Sally decides to ask Pablo for tango lessons afterward. He is initially disinterested until he finds out she is a filmmaker. "I've always wanted to be in films," says the thirty-something Pablo. The forty-something woman counters, "I've always wanted to be a dancer." A deal is eventually struck: he will teach her tango lessons, and she will have him star in her film. Their motivations in striking this bargain are evident in the literature they read as they separately soak in bathroom tubs in mirror-imaging shots: he reads a book on Brando; she reads Martin Buber's 1923 philosophical treatise on relationships, *I and Thou*.

The story is punctuated by headings that mark various episodes as "lessons," punning on whether these are dance lessons or lessons about life. They document Sally's increasing obsession with the dance, the subtleties of the music, and her teacher. Disappointed with the criticisms mounted against her conception of *Rage* by her Hollywood backers (shooting the film in French rather than English would significantly reduce its target market; casting a legless man would immediately decrease the pool of possible actors), Sally now decides to abandon her project in order to make a more personal film about the tango. Thus begins the complicated dance of advances and retreats between the two strong-willed individuals. In one emotionally charged scene, they mutually accuse each other of using the other to fulfill their fantasies. The reconciliation is prompted by Sally, who slightly deforms the biblical story of Jacob wrestling with the angel to become an eloquent appeal for reconciliation. Once again, it is Sally, the masculinized woman who moves, and it is he, the feminized hypermasculinized object of desire, who reacts. However, when they meet underneath Delacroix's painting of Jacob wrestling with the angel, it is Pablo who assumes the position of the angel and invites Sally to take the position of Jacob—their positions ambiguously meshing together the acts of wrestling and embracing, a poetic crystallization of the dynamic that Stanley Cavell terms the "comedy of remarriage."[28] The twelve lessons spiral toward a conclusion in which the relational dynamics shift. Sally demands that if Pablo is to star in her film, it is his turn to follow her. To signal the renewal of their relationship, she baptizes him using a few drops from a fountain, and he reciprocates. Then, claiming for herself the role of a virtual John the Baptist, she immerses her entire face in fountain, as if to leave behind their past history of pain. Yet things are not so easily resolved. When he refuses to reenact their tearful recognition of mutuality via the spiritual temperament of Jewishness, interpreting his shedding a tear as a potential threat to his masculinity, she threatens to replace him with another actor. As the film winds down, it is now he who complains that she is not "with him" when she directs, and it is he who expresses the fear of being swept away with no trace of his ever having lived. In turn, it is she who reassures him that the way she loves him entails looking at him and framing him through film, it is she who serenades him, implicitly reassuring him of some measure of immortality through her film and through their relationship.

The movie was much maligned, mainly by male critics, as an exercise in narcissism. Potter not only directs, writes, dances, and acts, but she also sings one of her own musical compositions in the penultimate scene, in which she reassures Pablo of her love and they dance their last tango by the moonlit river. The assumption of multiple roles is not unusual—Kenneth Branagh often does it in his own films. Yet the brunt of the accusations seemed to lie, once again, in the issue of credibility. The love affair, these critics protested, was not believable mainly because Potter is not *attractive* enough to be cast in that role. Berardinelli writes, "One of Potter's most egregious errors is casting herself as the lead. This is her acting debut—not only is she ineffective, but she has no screen presence whatsoever."[29] Jonathan Williams is more blunt about what "screen presence" entails: "Call me conventional, but I have to see some obvious physical beauty and energy in a woman onscreen for me to think that another man could fall in love with her. Even though this might be based on reality, I still had trouble believing he would be attracted to her."[30]

That accusation could certainly not be leveled against Saura's *Tango*, which is more conventional in its casting of the darkly beautiful type characteristic of the tango. Once again, the plot outlines of this movie may also be quickly summarized. *Tango* commences with a voiceover by Mario Suarez (Miguel Angel Sola), a choreographer–director reminiscing over his lost love. It is not clear whether the tango lyrics that capture his obsession with the missing woman are diegetic or not, but they eloquently convey his nostalgia and longing for Laura Fuentes (Cecilia Narova). When she returns to reclaim a necklace she had left behind, he attempts to win her back but fails miserably as she repulses him both verbally and physically. The larger context is that Suarez is charged with revisualizing Argentine national history through its national dance, the tango; yet the richness of the tango enables it to become a vehicle for both the personal and national traumas of Argentinians.

When a Mafioso who owns 50 percent of the shares of Mario's show, Angelo Larroca (Juan Luis Gallardo), suggests that Mario give his girlfriend, Elena Flores (Mia Maestro), an audition, the director ends up passionately entranced with the twenty-three-year-old beauty. He not only gives her a lead role, but he also, despite his former wife's warning and Angelo's declaration that he will kill her if she ever leaves him, eventually invites Elena to move in with him. The scene is thus set for playing out yet another archetypal theme of the tango: the love triangle, seething with jealousy, passion, and the threat of violence, particularly against women.

Since Mario's leg was injured by a passing car, unlike Fred Astaire, he cannot woo Elena with singing and dancing. Instead, he lavishes on her the insights of an older, mature artist and a man shadowed by sadness and loneliness, aware of his fragility and seeking love: "I feel energetic as a boy and want to act like it. . . . I enjoy a girl of eighteen. Is that unseemly? Where are my youthful illusions? I feel my life is superficial and that I'm just trying to avoid sinking in the muck." After initially resisting his invitation to stay with him that night, Elena eventually returns to break his imaginative reveries at three o'clock in the morning. She declares her break from Larocca, the Mafioso, ironically by singing the very song that marked the beginning of the movie.

Tango is less a plot-driven movie than a series of vivid, imaginative forays into the emotional realms of the dance. There are two dance sequences which are particularly noteworthy: one is imagined by Suarez during the lonely hours when he wishfully creates a script in which Elena returns to him; the other is presented for initial viewing to the producers of the show. I shall reserve detailed discussion in chapter 6, where I discuss attempts to rework boundaries of gender, race, class, sexuality, and nationality in films, of which this movie is a key example.

Both *Tango* and *The Tango Lesson* do explore the possibility of males dancing with each other. In *The Tango Lesson*, this is done more in the spirit of camaraderie and the mutual exploration of steps, as Sally, the director, watches. In *Tango*, under the watchful direction of Mario, the dances typically begin with Busby Berkeley-type formations. In one such striking example, half the screen is occupied by men dressed in white against a dark backdrop; the other half is filled by men dressed in black against a luminous white background. The two groups eventually mingle before the main pair takes center stage—a man dressed in black who plays the masculinized role of leading, and a man dressed in white who enacts the feminized role of following, though with powerful kicks that seem to defy gravity. The result is a more energetic, adversarial look—one probably close to one of the dance's original forms, which was danced by two men who challenged and dueled with each other—perhaps a defense measure set up to counter the shock of two male bodies locked in the embrace characteristic of the tango.

The tango, with its intensity, suffering, and unhappiness, is perhaps furthest away from the temperament of the Astaire-Rogers musicals. Unflinchingly Argentinean, the stories inspired by the tango reflect relationships that are edgy and frayed. Roger Ebert claims, "With the tango you never get the feeling the dancers have just met. They have a long history together, and not necessarily a happy one; they dance as a challenge, a boast, a taunt, a sexual put-down. It is the one dance where the woman gives as good as she gets, and the sexes are equal."[31] Such a statement strikes me as a little too optimistic. Nevertheless, both *The Tango Lesson* and *Tango* attest to the innumerable complex ways in which women (and men) are both allowed and disallowed access to realms of power enabled by the tango.

SHALL WE DANCE? (1997) AND *DANCE WITH ME* (1998)

At first glance, *Shall We Dance?* and *Dance with Me* seem fashioned from the same mold. They are both about the process of learning how to dance ballroom competitively within a studio context. They both populate the narrative with stock characters such as the matronly client who dreams of doing lifts, the aging studio owner who loses his competitive edge, the not-so-slim female instructor determinedly in search of a dance partner, the gangly student with a crush on his attractive but unreachable teacher, and the dance teacher whose life is so driven by the desire to win top honors in competitions that she becomes robotic and inhumane. Though both have comedic elements, they are principally melodramatic in character, unlike *Strictly Ballroom*, whose satirical and zany elements set it apart. Both declare themselves heirs to the Astaire-Rogers tradition by culminating in dance competitions in which everyone dresses like Fred and Ginger.

Yet a more in-depth look reveals them to be very different. *Shall We Dance?*, a Japanese production, is less a conventional romance than the story of a middle-aged man's search for freedom in a society regimented by rules. Paul Tatara adds, "It isn't really fair to suggest that the movie's main subject is dance, though. As much as anything else, it's about the healing powers (and poetry) of simple self-expression."[32] Steve Rhodes enthusiastically writes, "Although it is a descendant of the Fred Astaire and Ginger Rogers movies as well as the more recent *Strictly Ballroom*, the movie takes an approach so fresh and charming that it is easy to forget the formula roots of its plot. More than just a romantic comedy, it is a film of self-awakening and self-actualization."[33]

The film begins with a prologue (added to the shortened U.S. version, but not existent in the original Japanese version)[34] that explains how the expression of affection in public, even among married couples in Japan, is scandalous. Dancing, aligned with the expression of sexuality and the erotic, even among married couples, leaves them vulnerable to scandal. Dancing with a stranger, because of the close proximity it demands, is considered even worse so that taking dance lessons is tantamount to taking on a mistress. As Roger Ebert aptly phrases it, "Japan is in some ways still a Victorian society, which makes its eroticism more intriguing. Repression, guilt, and secrecy are splendid aphrodisiacs. Sugiyama creeps up the staircase like a man sneaking into a brothel, and enters a brightly lit room, where other students are already taking their lessons."[35]

The plot of *Shall We Dance?* can be sketched as follows. Shohei Sugiyama is a faithful middle-aged husband to Masako (Hideko Hara) and devoted father to a teenaged daughter. He seems to lead the perfect life, with an ideal family, a house (something quite rare in Japan, at his age), and a progressive career. He also seems to fit all the categories of perfection within this small universe: he comes home regularly after work, resisting invitations to stay late drinking with colleagues; he awakens before everyone else has in order to cook himself breakfast because the commute to the office demands this type of schedule; he has no vices. Yet something seems amiss.

Sugiyama takes the same train every night with clockwork precision. One night, he happens to gaze outside the train's doors and glimpses a delicate-looking beauty staring sadly out of a window of a ballroom dance studio. Every night thereafter, he looks for a glimpse of her. One night, he impulsively dashes out of the train. After many hesitations and numerous backward and sideways glances to make sure no one sees him, Sugiyama enters the studio, hilariously shoved in by an overweight, part-time female dance instructor who sweeps into the studio like a force of nature. Entranced by his divine apparition now in three-dimensional proximity, Sugiyama is tempted to take private lessons from Mai Kishikawa (Tamiyo Kusakari). However, because the price of private lessons is prohibitive, he opts for group lessons with a kindly older woman, Tamako Tamura (Reiko Kusamura), and gradually develops friendships with a cast of characters who are stock archetypes in dance studios. Among these are the heavyset diabetic Tanaka (Hiromasa Taguchi), whose doctor recommended dancing as exercise and whose emotional vulnerabilities are clearly evident; Sugiyama's coworker, Mr. Aoki (Naoto Takenaka), a balding systems analyst who transforms into a fiery Latin lover when he dons a frizzy wig and begins to rumba, fantasizing himself to be Donnie Burns, a former Latin champion;

and Toyoko Takahashi (Eriko Watanabe), an aging and plump female dance instructor determined to find a dance partner but who has difficulty keeping one because of her propensity for caustic comments.

Sugiyama struggles to overcome not only his physical awkwardness but also his shyness. The shame of his "unmanly" aspirations leads him to keep his lessons a secret. Probably the film's most important insight is ethnographic, as it is shot from a Japanese perspective. As Stephen Hunter observes, "The man who wants to dance but can't is not only middle class, middle-aged, repressed, shy and full of body-shame, but he's also Japanese, and formed by one of the most rigid of social codes."[36] Sugiyama's initial motivation for taking lessons is his fascination with Mai, but when she rudely and coldly rejects his offer of a dinner date, he continues dancing and slowly falls in love with dancing. He eventually becomes one of Toyoko's partners for an amateur competition and trains heavily, at no charge, with Mai, a former high-level professional competition dancer, a semifinalist in Blackpool, England, the world's most prestigious site of ballroom dance competitions.

Mai's characterization, compared with Shohei's wife, Masako (Hideko Hara), as well as Tamako Tamura, juxtaposes the three kinds of femininities Japanese society sets up as contrasting ideals. Mai is elegant and composed, always in control, similar to a general giving orders, and adept at setting up barriers between herself and others. One of the comical and enlightening scenes of the film occurs when Sugiyama finally has her in his arms for his first training session in preparation for the competition. Because his first step is hesitant, she stops and declares, "A weak first step transmits nothing"—which could have been a line from Sun Tzu's "The Art of War." Her function within the narrative is that of a muse as well as a mentor. Embittered by her loss during the Blackpool competition (as well as her partner's failure or desire not to protect her when she fell), along with her father's withdrawal of support from her, she is forced to teach at his school to support herself. Mai eventually confesses to Shohei that working with him and Toyoko renewed her enthusiasm for competitions, and revealed to her how solitary and selfish she had been in her partner dancing (which turns out to be the reason why her partner refused to protect her during the accident at Blackpool).

Masako is the typical Japanese housewife: cute, nonthreatening, neither lithe nor obese. Rather than confront her husband about his increasing late nights out and the perfume she smells on his clothes, she hires a private detective to find out whether Sugiyama is having an affair. She is purely economically dependent on her husband, and does not seem to have any power to convince him to do anything. It takes their daughter taking them forcefully by the hand and demanding that Shohei dance with his wife for the foundations of the marriage to be restored. Ultimately, Masako, consistent with her general characterization, self-sacrificially encourages Shohei to attend Mai's farewell party in order to dance with her.

Tamako, the older dance teacher, functions as a mother figure and a sage. She diplomatically comes up with the suggestion of doing group classes rather than private lessons when she senses Sugiyama's hesitations concerning the economic burden of taking private lessons. Slim and charming, she nevertheless knows that she is not an erotic object for most men in Japanese culture because of her age. Generous to a fault, she volunteers to train Shohei and Toyoko in preparation for the standard divisions of the competition without charging them. She also pairs Toyoko with Mr. Aoki for the Latin segment when she realizes that matching them would solve many of their problems concerning finding appropriate dance partners. Sensing that working with Mai would motivate Sugiyama to work even more arduously, she tactfully inquires whether Mai would be willing to function as Shohei's coach—an offer and plea Mai responds to with a slight smile. It is Tamako who utters the movie's title, which is derived from the 1956 movie *The King and I*, where the King (Yul Brynner) and Anna (Deborah Kerr) join hands and ecstatically whirl around the room. (There is also a Fred Astaire-Ginger Rogers movie titled *Shall We Dance?* which is about Linda Keene, a.k.a. Linda Thompson (Rogers) and a man, Petrov, a.k.a. Peter P. Peters of Pittsburgh (Astaire), who are both ensnared by the trappings of image. There is no direct link between the two movies that emerges from the production history of the later Japanese version.) Tamako also teaches Sugiyama that dance is "more than steps," and that the most important thing to do is to dance for the sheer joy of it; she again smilingly reminds him of these before he steps out onto the floor during the competition. Like Mai, she is also a working woman, though the film skips over the issue of the economic hierarchy at a typical studio, and whether because she is not the owner's daughter, or a high-level competitor, her wages would be significantly less than Mai's. Her willingness to train Sugiyama and his partner for competition without pay, given the realities of ballroom studio pay, thus mark her as a virtual martyr.

Shohei Sugiyama's masculinity is best sketched alongside the other men. Though Sugiyama is also initially clumsy and socially awkward like Tanaka, the obese diabetic, he does not bawl and shed tears like a child when he is insulted. Unlike Mr. Aoki, who is both hyperbolically masculinized during his Latin routines (with the body revealing outfits and the testosterone-dripping facial expressions, sounds, and gestures typical of Latin Dancesport) and in constant danger of being feminized (because of his small frame; his exaggeratedly sharp turns as he walks, as if he were still doing rumba turns; his proneness to fits of hysteria and mania), Sugiyama is consistently elegantly dressed, reserved, and temperate, even when he is insulted by the very woman he admires. He is probably as close to a Japanese version of Fred Astaire as one can get. Mr. Aoki's sexuality ambiguously hangs in between heterosexual and homosexual, as revealed in one humorous scene in the men's bathroom. Sugiyama and Aoki are shown practicing the basic ballroom frame. Aoki not only takes the follower's (female's) position in the frame; he also uses one of his hands to touch Sugiyama's buttocks, perhaps adjusting for a better posture (which simultaneously places him in the masculinized position as the more experienced dancer, but leaves the question of possible latent homosexual tendencies open). Even more importantly and comically, Aoki pretends to faint—a typical feminized gesture aligned with hysteria, a disease overwhelmingly categorized as "female disorder," leaving Sugiyama with the sole responsibility of holding him up. Repeatedly, Sugiyama emerges as a gallant man—one who does his best to support and protect his partner during competition.

Ultimately perhaps the closest tie between this Japanese film and the American Astaire-Rogers musicals is formal rather than thematic. Suo, like Astaire, prefers to have the camera to the side, keeping its distance, so as to capture the whole dance; occasionally, though, he uses close-ups to underscore the drama or the emotional complexities of the characters.

In contrast, the links binding *Dance With Me* to the Astaire-Rogers musicals and other more recent offshoots are so obvious that it is difficult not to begin with the most overt connections. Donna Bowman remarks, "Director Randa Haines . . . and screenwriter Daryl Matthews, who is also one of the film's choreographers, stick close to the spirit of the movies they're imitating—*Strictly Ballroom* and *Shall We Dance?*, most notably—and in their best moments they deliver the same *Top Hat*-meets-*Tin Cup* thrills. . . . For a shamelessly small, sentimental project like this, the formulaic plot itself is as comfortable as one of Fred Astaire's worn-out tap shoes."[37] Nevertheless, Kay Dickinson differentiates *Dance With Me* from one of its most obvious points of reference: "The spangled campness of its most obvious precedent, *Strictly Ballroom*, is replaced by a sweet earnestness that caters particularly for Latin-dance neophytes."[38]

Dance With Me thus returns to the old familiar and successful formula of making the sentimental love affair the central fulcrum of the narrative, infusing it with some elements of gravity but remaining predominantly lighthearted, as signaled formally by its predominant use of soft- and high-key lighting, which sets the movie's intimate mood. The central characters in this story all suffer from various emotional complexes, which, in this simple formulaic story, the joy of dancing eventually heals. Ruby (Vanessa L. Williams, former Ms. America-turned singer-turned actress) is a stunningly beautiful former DanceSport champion who has been disappointed in love by her former partner, who sired her child, and left her while she was pregnant; consequently, she repulses all romantic involvement and dreams only of making a comeback. Rafael Infante (Chayanne, Puerto Rican singing idol and television star) is an attractive young Cuban whose mother dies and who longs to know his father; to do that, he must leave behind the town of Santiago, where he is much loved. John Burnett (Kris Kristofferson) is the burned-out owner of a fading dance studio in Houston, whose aspirations seem only to lie in trading in his dance shoes for a fishing pole. Bea Johnson (Joan Plowright) is an overweight, fun-loving senior citizen who depends on the Houston studio to rekindle her passion for life.

Like an Astaire-Rogers movie, the plot begins with misunderstanding and annoyance between the future lovers. When Rafael shows up at the Houston studio at the invitation of its owner, John, he is immediately drawn to Ruby but is puzzled at how she can disconnect dancing from music, which, in his view, renders her dancing "stiff" and lifeless. She is irritated at his unsolicited advice and immediately emphasizes her professional status as a dancer to put him in his place as a mere handyman in the studio. When they finally go out on a date and first attempt to do a mambo, she tries to instruct him, using terms like "heel ball change," which results in Rafael simply clumsily stepping on her feet. She excuses herself and returns to find Rafael gleefully and with joyful abandon, moving sinuously with another attractive young woman. Feeling insulted, she storms out, leaving him to walk home.

Once again, the movie hinges on the binary dichotomy set up between simulated dancing, done by professionals in order to win championships, with no connection to music or community, and genuine dancing, done principally by amateurs, who have not severed the spontaneous pleasures of dancing from the primitive beats of music shared with the collective. Interestingly, even critics adhere to this binary. Barbara Schulgasser writes, "While Ruby's professional partner, Julian (Rick Valenzuela [a pro in real life]) dances spasmodically as if he means to throw his limbs out of his sockets, Chayanne's body [an amateur in real life as well] is easy and loose when he moves to the Latin rhythms."[39]

Disturbingly though, the film attaches the ability to move to music as an inherent, ethnic property—a position that both valorizes Hispanic culture but still marks it as an exotic other—a nobly savage culture, much like in *Dirty Dancing: Havana Nights*. In a conversation that ensues after the disastrous nightclub date, Ruby says accusingly, "I thought you couldn't dance!" Rafael counters smoothly, "I'm Cuban. Of course, I can dance."

That Ruby is African American rather than white sets up a complex racial dynamic. Clearly, she is marked as American, yet she occupies that liminal space, occupied similarly by other African American actresses like

Halle Berry, in between blackness and whiteness. With her comparatively lightly complected skin and her hair dyed in streaks of blonde, she moves across realms of blackness and whiteness and the camera gazes voyeuristically in particular at her flashing legs as she practices. Rafael, though he is from Cuba, is similarly lighter in skin color than the rest of his countrymen (hardly surprising, as his father, John Burnett, is white). Though his accent sets him apart, he converses easily enough in English to become believable as a first-generation immigrant. Like Ruby, he, too, is eroticized: in the famous bathroom kissing scene, he wears little more than a towel, and the camera lingers on his bare chest. Both major characters thus still essentially partake in an aesthetic of whiteness, while being aligned with nonwhiteness. At the further ends of the racial continuum are the extremely ethereal, white, and blonde Patricia (Jane Krakowski), who is ballet trained and does cabaret dancing, which is characterized by lifts (as opposed to Ruby, who does the more grounded, seductive Latin dances), and Julian (Rick Valenzuela), Ruby's ex-partner and ex-paramour, who has a dark complexion and is stereotypically seething with machismo and egotism as the quintessential professional Latin dancer, sporting a ponytail and wearing the tight-fitting outfits characteristic of the sport. All the characters in this story are unambiguously marked as heterosexual—something actually contrary to particularly the real Latin dance competitive scene, which is dominated by gay men.

One of the favorite myths of Hollywood cinema is that class ultimately does not matter, and this film eventually touts the same party line. There are initial indications of tension due to class differences, such as Ruby's sharp delineation of her status as a professional dance instructor and Rafael's as a mere handyman, as well as John's initial vehement denial of his paternity of Rafael, which hints at his family's disapproval of his marrying a poor Cuban girl. Nevertheless, these seem superficial to the plot and are easily overcome in the film's concluding shot, where everyone, it appears, lives happily ever after. Both Ruby and Rafael are shown leading a group of dancers at the studio, which implies Rafael's inheritance of it, Ruby and Rafael's marriage, and John's decision after all not to shut the studio, which seems resurrected. Interestingly, though the film begins with glorifying Cuba's poor, Rafael and Ruby do not return there, but stay on in the United States. Like *Dirty Dancing: Havana Nights*, *Dance With Me* romanticizes Cuba and separates this mythic Cuba from its social, political, and economic realities.

Yet the ultimate obscuring of class issues lies in the turning point of the film. In Las Vegas, Ruby and Julian have danced magnificently despite their arguments and exchanged insults, hissed between smiling, clenched teeth. The last dance is the rumba, the dance of love. Ruby, suddenly realizing what her impending loss of Rafael would mean to her, breaks away from their set routine and begins to search the crowd for Rafael, swaying to the sultry music in a manner that recalls the intimate way in which they had earlier danced. An eyeline match unites the lovers, and he returns the gesture. As Julian pulls Ruby back into their routine, she resists, until magically, a sudden cut replaces Julian with Rafael, which moves Ruby to dance even more expressively and intensely. Then another cut moves Julian back into the picture, revealing the earlier sequence to be Ruby's fantasy, which is what enables her to perform to her utmost and eventually achieve her dream of winning the championship. Ironically and predictably, her dreams of professional success and economic prosperity now seen hollow and she seems dazed as she examines a contract enthusiastically offered to her by an agent. Rafael gently lays his hand on her shoulder and they again begin dancing joyfully together—leading the crowd to gather around them and away from the showoff Julian, who, once he realizes no one is looking at him and his partner, abruptly stops dancing and stalks off.

It is clear that Ruby's repeated lapses in concentration during the rumba routine in an actual competition would have rapidly resulted in their loss, so authenticity is an issue in the film's climactic scene. Yet more importantly, the movie again sets up another simplistic binary dichotomy: one either pursues professional and economic success at the expense of personal happiness, or one places one's trust in true love, regardless of professional and economic consequences. True love transcends all class boundaries, and somehow magically solves any economic difficulties.

Remarkably, like Astaire-Rogers musicals, *Dance With Me* is sexually restrained save for a passionate kiss that Ruby aborts. It enacts a retrospective disjunction of "dancing" from "dirty" and a return to the old-fashioned notion that expressive dancing is not a prelude to sex, but is sex, or something far finer than physical sex—something very much in keeping with Astaire's preference for dances as avenues for seduction and amorous engagement rather than torrid love scenes. Astaire's reluctance to do all-out romantic scenes may be traced initially to the fact that his first serious stage partner was his sister, Adele; when Adele married and left him without a partner, he teamed up with the lithe and voluptuous Claire Luce. Nevertheless, Luce reminisces that she had to encourage him to overcome his inhibitions: "Come on, Fred, I'm not your sister, you know." And even when he had gotten more comfortable with love scenes, Astaire never conceived of himself as a "true romantic lead" and had a severe antipathy to mushy dialogues and clichés as passionate kisses: "Saying 'I love you' was the job of our dance routines," he explains.[40]

There are other subtle and very clever ways in which the film is aligned with the tradition of the American musical. As Rafael is accidentally doused by sprinklers, he does a comic rendition of Gene Kelly's hopping and stomping routine in *Singing in the Rain*. In addition, in a brief shot shown with the end credits, Rafael is shown dancing with his mop, much as Astaire had often done with other inanimate objects, such as hat racks. Finally, during Ruby and Chayanne's dance of reunion at the night club, one section of their dance has them putting their foreheads together as their bodies continue to undulate. That part is brief, but it has clear affinities to the carioca, which was first performed by Astaire and Rogers in their screen debut as a couple (but in minor roles) in *Flying Down to Rio*.

Briefly described, the basic carioca step is a to-and-fro tilt with foreheads touching, pelvises aligned, and with the hands clasped overhead. The trickiness of the dance demanded that each partner do a complete turn without breaking head contact. Hermes Pan, its choreographer, got his inspiration from the lyrics of the song, "Two heads together/ They say/ Are better than one/ Two heads together/ That's how/ The dance is begun." The carioca was a fast tango with similarities to the maxixe (also called the "tango *Brésilienne*"), which Vernon Castle had attempted to introduce to an American audience in 1914. Though the maxixe never captured the public imagination, the carioca did, and dance schools made it part of their curriculum due to public demand.[41] It is thus hardly surprising that one finds its imprint even in contemporary choreography. Indeed, Susanne Topper points out the direct correlation between the popularity of Astaire's choreographed dances in *The Gay Divorcee*, the continental and the carioca, and their subsequent inclusion in ballroom dance school curricula: "Both of these dance crazes impelled countless people to enrich ballroom dance schools as they strived to learn the steps."[42]

CONCLUSION

Contemporary films that use ballroom or DanceSport as a motif for the unfolding of their narratives clearly but in different ways pronounce themselves as heirs to the Astaire-Rogers cinematic legacy. In these musicals, the couple is usually costumed according to stereotypical gender characterizations: she is swathed in soft and flowing feminine glamour, while he is tailored in elegant masculine attire. Similarly, their mannerisms and patterns of interaction fall within the range of what is considered normal—that is, within a heterosexual spectrum. Though Rogers has a wide gamut of tonalities and expressions, they all remain safely heterosexually feminine, whether they be irritated, saucy, or innocent. In like manner, Astaire, particularly when set against his generally less physically appealing rivals, moves easily within the masculine modes of pronouncing, demanding, pursuing, and asserting. Nevertheless, there is a sense in which while they reinscribe conventional mores concerning appearances, Astaire and Rogers, in conjunction with each other, allow for some exploration of androgeneity and unconventional mutuality. As Martha Nochimson points out, "The stereo-typical male-female domination/submission mode is scrambled in their films. The Astaire/Rogers characters are equally assertive, witty, spirited, and playful in pursuing their desires, speaking their minds, and asserting competency as well as sexuality."[43]

All the contemporary films I have discussed in this chapter partake in essentially the same dynamic, allowing for varying degrees of porousness, particularly in the connections between gender and power. One significant difference that seems to run through the majority of the contemporary films is that the women no longer have to be as beautiful or as elegant as Ginger to be credible as romantic objects. *Dirty Dancing*'s Baby is cute and appealing, but certainly not a ravishing beauty; *Strictly Ballroom*'s Fran, though she loses her thick lenses and adopts more conventional feminine attire as she metamorphoses into Scott's partner, never comes close to Ginger's style and classiness. Nevertheless, there still are limits: Sally Potter's acting in the movie she directed, scripted, danced in, and sang in was generally interpreted as a sign of hubris, and male critics in particular castigated her for her casting of herself as the lead because she was not "attractive" enough to be believable as a romantic object for the much younger and very virile Pablo Veron. Despite this, *Tango Lesson* distinguishes itself as a bold experiment in exploring what an authoritative and creative female gaze of desire entails. *Shall We Dance?* is a bit of an anomaly from the rest because the potential or Platonic love story is not as central as the search for individual expression and freedom.

Another common motif binding Astaire-Rogers films to these con-temporary offshoots is the link between the spontaneity of dance and a certain gifted primitivism. Many of Astaire's dance sequences have him acting as though he cannot help but move to music once the beat begins; it is as if a divine force possesses him and moves his limbs almost against his will, which he eventually joyfully surrenders to. For example, in *The Gay Divorcee*, Astaire is determined to find the elusive Rogers though she has left no trace of her whereabouts. Astaire's solo song and dance number "A Needle in the Haystack" explores his anticipated difficulties in locating the mysterious woman. Mueller eloquently describes this particular num-ber: "As he sinks into thought—reflecting, no doubt, on the difficult quest before him—he is amused to find that his right foot (indeed, his whole leg) has begun to dance. . . . Gradually the rest of his body joins in, pro-pelling him at one point in a goofy little waddle . . . and then finally into movements that are so broad that they cannot be contained on the hearth and carry him into the center of the room."[44]

This myth of primitivism continues in contemporary films, some-times acquiring the added veneer of ethnic exoticism that verges on a type of biological or cultural determinism. Thus, *Dance With Me*'s Rafael and *Dirty Dancing: Havana Nights*'s Javier are spectacular dancers simply because they are Cuban; they do not need formal instruction because by virtue of their racial heritage, they automatically know what genuine dancing looks and feels like. What results is a nostalgia for Cuba, devoid of its complex social, political, and economic histories. The films generally reinforce the racial aesthetics characteristic of typical DanceSport competitions, with whiteness being associated with ethereality and elegance, and nonwhiteness with seductiveness and primitivism. Though the central characters in *Dance With Me* (portrayed by Vanessa Williams and Chayanne) are nonwhite, they partake in an aesthetic of whiteness in a continuum that distinguishes between the ultra white (played by the balletic Jane Krakowski) and the irredeemably nonwhite (the one-dimensional evil ex-paramour played by Rick Valenzuela). Fran's Hispanic ethnicity, evidenced in her accent, the neighborhood in which she lives, and her non-English speaking family, mark her as an exotic other. Her father and grandmother, who are coded as noble savages by virtue of their inability to converse in English and their instinctive understanding of what dancing the paso doble entails, occupy an ambiguous position—simultaneously empowered and marginalized.

In terms of class, expertise in dance runs the gamut from the extremely poor (Johnny Castle in *Dirty Dancing;* Javier in *Dirty Dancing: Havana Nights*) to the middle class (Laura and Elena in *Tango*) to the generally privileged (Scott in *Strictly Ballroom*; Mai in *Shall We Dance?*; Ruby in *Dance With Me*). Astaire-Rogers musicals do not address the issue of class directly; if anything, they imply that everyone is uniformly wealthy, partying until the early morning hours in their gowns and tuxedos. Contemporary films address class issues, but generally tend to dismiss them as ultimately irrelevant or treat these as temporary obstacles that are overcome in the grand finale when love is the cure to everything. Similarly, though there are various types of masculinities and femininities depicted in these films, ranging from the simultaneously hypermasculinized and comically feminized Mr. Aoki to the clinically precise ice princess Mai in *Shall We Dance?*, or the cocky and vulnerable pretty boy, Pablo Veron, and equally cocky and vulnerable but more mature female director, Sally Potter, in *Tango Lesson*, all of these remain safely inscribed within the heterosexual mode of interaction. This is also very much in keeping with the heterosexual aesthetic DanceSport demands, even if the reality is that gay men heavily populate particularly the Latin dances.

One cinematic legacy Fred Astaire institutionalized is the drastic reduction of distracting shots such as those close-ups of disconnected dancing feet or reaction shots of an audience watching the dance. Astaire boldly pronounced, "Either the camera will dance or I will." Accordingly, he also insisted on a minimum of editorial cuts in the filming of his dances in order to ensure continuity and integrity.[45] This convention, for the most part, seems to have been lost in contemporary films. The closest to this is evidenced in Masayuki Suo's subtle camera work in *Shall We Dance?*, which tends to have the camera to the side, unobtrusively recording the dance and its mise-en-scène in long to medium shots, sometimes punctuated by close-ups for dramatic or emotional impact. But the majority of the films reinsert everything Astaire had cut out—even the boldly independent Sally Potter resorts to close-ups of legs flashing past each other and reaction shots of herself viewing Pablo Veron dance. Probably the most egregious deviation is Baz Luhrmann's *Strictly Ballroom*, which uses every camera trick imaginable to produce a form that is in conjunction with the frenzied, maddened, claustrophobic world obsessed with winning competitions that it depicts. Despite these deviations, these movies clearly and proudly align themselves with the glamour and enduring legend of the Astaire-Rogers cinematic tradition. In this way, they help propagate ballroom's prestigious reputation and informally boost, at the level of popular culture, DanceSport's bid to become a medaled Olympic sport. Their very ubiquity and variety, in terms of genre, as the appendix reveals, show the extent to which the mythology and aesthetic of ballroom/DanceSport has infiltrated the public imagination, both within the United States and internationally. From this larger cultural backdrop, we now move to a specific focus on the "art versus sport" debate that shadows the drive to the Olympics.

FOUR

Paving the Road to the Olympics

Staging and Financing the Olympic Dream

WHAT'S IN A NAME?:
BALLROOM DANCE OR DANCESPORT?

"The announcers were condescending and rude."

"Making a lame joke about Rita Moreno pulling a hamstring only shows their ignorance."

"We were verbally abused and molested."

"They diminished themselves in the eyes of many thousands of North American viewers, not only ballroom dancers."

"Shame on you, Bob Costas!"[1]

The above tirade of complaints regarding NBC's coverage of and commentary on DanceSport's debut as an officially recognized sport in the closing ceremonies of the Sydney Olympic Games in 2000 contextualizes this book, which deals with the transformation of ballroom dance as a recreational activity or art into a sport.

Nevertheless, the less than complimentary commentary was far from the only problem in the showcasing of DanceSport as an Olympic exhibition. As various participants attested, some of the difficulties included: (1) being prevented by security guards from testing the stage for a rehearsal before the actual show;[2] (2) the samba music, set for 180 beats per minute (as opposed to the competition format of 120 beats per minute), which was introduced to the dancers after a month of choreography without music; (3) the floor surface, a type of rubber matting designed to give athletes nonslip traction, but which tended to slow down dancers doing fast turns; and (4) the six-meter-high Kewpie dolls, which, together with one thousand dancers, necessitated a radical revision of the choreography to exclude all nontraveling sections. As dancer Don Herbison-Evans noted: "I do not know which idea came first: the 6 metre high dolls or the 1000 dancers, but whoever put these together missed the point of ballroom dancing. A lone dancer or even group of dancers often needs extra things to give their dance an energy lift: noisy shoes, exotic costumes, whatever. But Ballroom and Latin American dancing are not just about dancing, they are about the relationship between two people. This is its extra thing. Ballroom dancing does not need 10 [sic?] metre high dolls in principle, and in practice they were a disaster."[3]

"DanceSport" was the label introduced to designate a competitive and more athletic form of ballroom in order to set it apart from its more recreational and social counterpart, which is often stereotypically visualized as dancing by seniors. The difference between the two has been described thus: "When this self-expressive, free-flowing dance takes on a stricter format, follows a syllabus and specific steps and moves are judged by an international criteria, ballroom dancing becomes dance sport."[4] Yet to have ballroom authorized as a sport and to thus attract the funding, commercial sponsorship, and prestige that other Olympic sports have become, the promoters of DanceSport have also had to distance themselves from other analogies to dance, such as ballet and modern dance.

Although the term "DanceSport" has had some currency in Europe for years, it was only in 1989 that the International DanceSport Federation (IDSF), the governing body for amateur and professional competitive ballroom dancers, formerly known as the International Ballroom Dancing Federation, adopted its use in a quest for inclusion as a medalled sport by the International Olympic Committee (IOC).[5] Acknowledgement of the IDSF as a recognized federation and member of the IOC came on September 8, 1997—the first step toward full participation in the Olympics. Provisional recognition came on June 5, 1995, in a letter from IOC president Juan Antonio Samaranch to IDSF president Detlef Hegemann—which resulted in a media feeding frenzy. However, this did not mean an automatic pass to being recognized as a medal sport. What it accomplished was simply that IOC was recognized as an international body for governing DanceSport, empowering it to fashion the technical rules for competition in that sport. The recognition of the IDSF as a member of IOC was crucial because for two reasons. First, becoming a member of IOC is necessary in order to achieve full status as a medal sport. Second, IOC's vision of furthering sports at an international level is consonant with and advantageous to the IDSF. Nevertheless, advocacy for the Olympic status of DanceSport appeared to hinge on the sometimes nebulous factors of "general perception, equal participation for women, television appeal, and overall excitement."[6] Progress along these lines seemed readily visible in 1996, when the IDSF held its general meetings in Lausanne, the Netherlands, home base of the IOC, where Gilbert Felli, the most influential director of the IOC, addressed the assembly.[7] However, this success was eclipsed by continuing tensions between the IDSF, populated by amateurs, and the World Dance & Dance Sport Council (WD&DSC), composed of professional dance teaching organizations, coaches, and organizers. The rivalry hinged on which body should be the appropriate channel of communication and governance. In the visibly skewed framing of the problem by IDSF president Hegemann, the issue was that the IDSF was interested in the sport while the WD&DSC was simply interested in protecting its "livelihood and personal future."[8]

To resolve the controversy, Juan Antonio Samaranch, president of the IOC, declared that only the IDSF and its national member associations were the conduits authorized to set rules concerning DanceSport on its road to the Olympics.[9] Nevertheless, the most important development from the 1996 general meetings was that DanceSport had succeeded in gaining entry in the 1997 World Games in Lahti, Finland.[10] In April 1996, sloppy journalism resulted in the rumor that DanceSport would be an exhibition sport at the Atlanta Games, which again whipped up a controversy. Gilberto Felli, then IOC Sports Director, immediately sent Rudolf Baumann a message clarifying that the use of DanceSport as a demonstration or exhibition at Atlanta was not authorized.[11] To improve relations between the competing organizations, a meeting was held in Brussels on April 21, 1996. The most important development at that meeting was the general agreement to integrate the professionals and amateurs into a single competitive group, with the Swiss being the first to experiment with proposals on how to accomplish this goal.[12] Finally, also in 1996, the IDSF received ten thousand dollars from the IOC as a "welcome gift." It used the money for drug testing for the first time at the World Championships, held in the Netherlands on May 18, 1996. That none of the participants tested positive for prohibited substances again boosted its profile.[13]

The year 1997 proved to be a banner year of successes and conflicts. The competition between the IDSF and the WD&DSC flared up again when the WD&DSC proposed a 50/50 integration with the IDSF, resulting in the WD&DSC submitting its own letter bidding once again for an authorized position with the IOC. Contributing to the upheaval was President Detlef Hegemann's sudden announcement of his plans for retirement. Nevertheless, this was also the year in which the IDSF announced its signing of an eleven-year contract with the world-renowned sport management group, International Management Group (IMG), and its affiliate television company, Trans World International (TWI). This resulted in major format changes as a result of the agreement with IMG. The Russian amateur and professional organizations, following the general trend, also unified under a single body, strengthening the IDSF. Yet the biggest achievement of 1997 was the movement from being "provisionally" accepted into "full" IOC recognition.[14]

In 1998, in a move long foreseen, the IDSF removed the words "amateur" and "professional" from its statutes, and the WD&DSC finally became accepted as an associate member of the IDSF. DanceSport secured a place in the Asian Games held in Bangkok on December 7, 1998, thus enhancing its visibility. Meanwhile, clearly marking its steps toward Olympic recognition, the IDSF decreed that competition rules must be determined on the basis of promoting a "sports image" as opposed to a "performing arts image." Unfortunately, all that good press was counterbalanced by proverbial dirty linen being aired in public as the circumstances surrounding the sudden resignation of Detlef Hegemann and his subsequent attempt at reelection were publicized. To make things worse, the German federation (the Deutscher Tanzverein, or DTV) boycotted the IDSF and refused to host the IDSF World Latin Championships in the attempt to coerce the reinstatement of Hegemann. The controversy climaxed with Rudolf Baumann defeating Detlef Hegemann in the IDSF presidential election. To save face and to heal divisions, Detlef Hegemann accepted the newly created position of Honorary Life President. With these upheavals finally coming to rest, the first IMG-hosted event in the United States posted tremendous ratings and was a clear success.[15]

In April 1999, the United States Ballroom Dancers Association (USABDA), which was founded in 1965 for the same aim of promoting ballroom's Olympic status, was granted affiliate membership by the United States Olympic Committee (USOC), thus opening the way for amateurs to compete alongside professionals. As IDSF President Rudolf Bauman announced, "The most important change in 1999 will be the complete deletion of the word 'Amateur' from our statutes. . . . What are the consequences of this major step? All DanceSport Competitors are 'Athletes.' "[16] The United States hosted its first event where both amateurs and professionals competed in Las Vegas on June 8, 1999. Coverage of the event was a landmark success, with the IMG competition landing primetime television coverage on NBC. Meanwhile, for political and tax reasons, the IDSF relocated its headquarters to Lausanne, Switzerland.[17]

In 2000 DanceSport was featured as an exhibition event, using up to five hundred DanceSport couples, at the closing ceremonies of the 27th Olympiad in Sydney, Australia.[18] But the real push was initially for the 2008 Olympics, when enthusiasts hoped that it would be a medalled competition. Delerine Munzeer of the *Sunday Observer* projected that although no events would be added to the 2004 Olympics in Greece, DanceSport will (hopefully) be included as an event in 2008.[19] Technically, under chapter 52 of the IOC chapter, sports must receive medal program inclusion for a minimum of seven years before the games begin. It also requires that a sport be practiced by men in seventy-five countries on four continents, and by women in forty countries on three continents. This meant that inclusion in both Sydney in 2000 and in Athens in 2004 was impossible not only because of time constraints, but also because the IDSF was still shy of the required number of countries required for medal inclusion. In 2000, the *Daily Telegraph* in Australia reported that the IOC rejected Dancesport for inclusion as a medalled event. While this received a lot of refractory responses it is important to keep the larger perspective in mind: no single new sport was included for the Olympics in Athens, neither rugby, nor cricket nor DanceSport. It is equally important to note that there are several international federations that have been recognized by the IOC, but do not yet sponsor medalled events. Among these are the World Amateur Golf Council, Fédération Mondiale de Karate, Fédération Internationale de Polo, International Racquetball Federation, International Rugby Football Board, World Squash Federation, and sixteen other federations. Despite the fact that golf and squash are incontestably classified as sports have the necessary infrastructure in place, and have immense numerical and geographical coverage, they are still not part of the medal program of the Olympics.[20]

In keeping with this general trend, on August 28, 2002, the IOC executive board recommended that requests by DanceSport and thirteen other sports for admission to medal status in the 2008 Olympics be denied. Nevertheless, it should be noted that the board also suggested removing a number of already approved events, such as baseball. As the USABDA's own website predicted, "The recommendation probably pushes forward to 2012 the earliest date DanceSport can hope for another try at gaining full Olympic status."[21] Nevertheless, the very same press releases softened the disappointing news by focusing on DanceSport's continuing participation in the World Games, an event held for recognized Olympic sports that have not yet achieved medal status. It also pointed out that though this ruling effectively rendered impossible DanceSport being a medalled event in 2008, it also gave the IDSF, for the first time, the authority to set forth specific requirements a sport must satisfy in order to qualify for medal status. A meeting between Rudolf Baumann (current IDSF president), Carlos Freitag (IDSF general secretary), Dr. Jacques Rogge (IOC president) and Gilbert Felli (IOC sport director) on October 4, 2002, in Lausanne was described as "very positive" and it was reported that the IOC had made "encouraging and constructive suggestions" concerning how best to enhance DanceSport's candidacy for medal status, supporting especially IDSF's television initiative, which was aimed at transmitting televised DanceSport to 150 million homes around the world.[22] Johannes Biba, the IDSF communications director, proved himself a master at rhetorical wizardry as he alchemically changed a "negative" into a "positive." He emphasized that DanceSport, among only ten that "survived the Commission's scrutiny and radical cuts," while it is not recommended for admission in the 2008 Beijing Olympics, is clearly "eligible" for future medal status if it can "add value in terms of participation and media coverage." Among the new criteria for inclusion were the emphasis on youth and development, increased participation at various levels, the use of already existing facilities as opposed to new expensive ones, and the noninclusion of "mind-sports" or sports with a regional rather than international appeal. Biba rosily concluded that the IOC essentially ended up recommending that DanceSport advocates simply keep doing what they are essentially already doing very well: "These new criteria give DanceSport clear and growing advantages. With big growth in participation amongst the youth of the world, a newly-enhanced IDSF Membership Commission that is reaching out enthusiastically to many new countries and a newly-strengthened Presidium; with no requirement for special construction or costly facilities; and with a dazzling program of television development—IDSF can deliver what the IOC wants."[23]

Unfortunately, much as the IDSF would like to present the story of the march to the Olympics as a united front, by late 2002 to early 2003 the old tensions between the professional (WD&DSC) and amateur (IDSF) groups of DanceSport again arose. A meeting held in London on October 13, 2002, revealed that truly forming a coalition is still fraught with difficulty. The IDSF's "best ever" offer to drop the title "IDSF" in favor of the title "World DanceSport Federation" (WDSF) to show the incorporation of the WD&DSC into the IDSF was met with "fear and suspicion" by the WD&DSC leaders and ultimately rejected. Though Baumann tried to differentiate between individual professionals and the current leadership of the WD&DSC, his frustration with the stalemate was clear, and he rhetorically sketched conflict between the opposing sides as a fight between traditionalists, who prefer to keep ballroom as a "performing art," versus the progressives, who see DanceSport as an "artistic sport." "It may come down to this: Those who see ballroom dancing exclusively as a performing art, with all of the culture and customs that entails, will never support unification with the IDSF. Those who see DanceSport as an artistic sport, as the modern expression of what we have all grown up with, with a contemporary culture and modern customs, will support the IDSF push for unification."[24] Nevertheless, it is important to note that the move to make ballroom dance into a sport is controversial, not only across the professional/amateur divide, but also among amateur enthusiasts themselves. Part of the issue is whether amateurs can truly attract television and media coverage, the way professionals can, or whether it is truly fair to place amateurs and professionals on the same floor at the same time: "Is it fair for professionals to be competing against amateurs? Or should it be an open field, where the best will represent their countries, which invariably implies the professionals will end up representing their countries?"[25] But there are other arguments posed by DanceSport competitors themselves. A random sampling of comments from *DanceSport Magazine*'s reader responses (posted on rec.arts.dance) to the IOC's rejection of the IDSF's application for full-member-sport status in 2008 produced the following responses. Ed Jay wrote in, "It is presumptuous to think that the inclusion of [DanceSport] in the Olympics would do anything to inspire the populace to take up partnership dancing. How is your flag twirling, syncopated swimming, etc., coming along?" Warren Dew, another reader, sounded a Cassandra-like warning: "The Olympics will take us down the road from the present highly developed art form to a splashy sideshow. The experience with figure skating shows that for judged Olympic sports, no technique is needed—just the showiest, splashiest tricks possible."[26]

To take away the brunt of these objections, Baumann characterized the goal of making DanceSport an Olympic medal sport as simply one among many, and emphasized that IDSF's current leadership is very much "concerned with the development of DanceSport in all its aspects."[27] In an earlier conciliatory attempt to reach out to the WD&DSC, though Rudi Hubert (IDSF general secretary) firmly and "unapologetically" rejected the concept of a straight 50/50 unification proposed by the WD&DSC in 1997, he sketched the outlines for a possible truce between the two factions: "It is however perfectly appropriate to have 50/50 arrangements when discussing joint projects aimed at integrating functions, for example, competition calendars, dress codes, age restrictions, [and] judging standards." Hubert thus rhetorically distinguished between practical governance in relation to specific events, in which democratic principles of representation could be effected, and more general symbolic and policy-oriented leadership, which he unambiguously wanted reserved for the IDSF.[28] Nevertheless, what is clear is that the issue of who best represents the interests of the DanceSport community as a whole is going to be an intrinsic and ongoing feature of the road to the Olympics.

In the remainder of this chapter, I examine how ballroom dancing is in the process of being rhetorically repackaged from being either a social pastime or an art form (modeled on other dances, such as ballet or modern) into a high-profile Olympic event. I pay particular attention to the rhetorical strategies used to authorize this type of dancing as a sport, and how, as such, it flirts with and regulates corporate sponsorship and advertising. In addition, I examine how rules govern what is considered appropriate masculine and feminine attire and demeanor (as related to race and class), as well as what criteria judges rely on in order to evaluate its desirable aesthetic and athletic masculine and feminine lines and attributes. For the most part, sources here are drawn from the Internet, where the outlines and most recent developments concerning the debate are more clearly tracked. For now, websites effectively constitute the primary texts for tracking DanceSport's evolution from recreation and social dance to competitive Olympic sport.

SPORT OR ART?

Debates over whether or not DanceSport is a sport have been as steamy as any physical contact sport. An illustration of one battlefront comes from David Watts, a West Australian columnist whose 1998 piece "Love of Sport Takes a High Dive" included the following often-quoted lines: "Can anyone tell me how it is possible to have solo synchronized swimming? Who does the solo synchronized swimmer synchronize with? . . . Is it the little green men who have so obviously inspired swimming officials to make synchronized swimming a sport? The same little green men have worked their evil way through rhythmic gymnastics, ballroom dancing and figure skating—all wonderful pastimes, but sport . . . I don't think so."[29]

The columnist was certainly not alone in his skepticism concerning DanceSport's viability as an Olympic sport. Several years later, there was little evidence of a change in perception: in 2001, Jonathan M. Bell declared that ballroom dancing is not a sport because "there isn't room for failure."[30] In Lausanne, where ballroom dancers showcased a demonstration of the tango, samba, cha-cha, rumba, and other steps in a bid to get the sport included in the 2004 Athens Olympics, one senior IOC member reportedly mumbled as he walked in halfway through the performance, "I can't believe I am watching this."[31]

A roundtable forum sponsored by the IOC on the sport-versus-art distinction produced little that could be used to produce practical policy. Though all agreed that both art and sport are crucial components in Olympic culture, and that sports are inherently artistic, not all arts are necessarily sporting. Though a number of the commentators attempted to define sport as opposed to art, all eventually arrived at a version of Justice Scalia's characterization of the indecent or pornographic: "I know it when I see it." On a loftier note, Carol Ann Letheren quoted Plato's remark that "the body must be trained for gymnastics and the soul for music." Nevertheless, she conceded that they are still different things: "An evening at the stadium is no replacement for an evening at the theater . . . or vice versa."[32] Charles Jencks made the recommendation to augment the current format of the Olympics with a "'Cultural Olympics' along the lines of what Coubertin envisaged."[33] Jencks was referring to the Baron de Coubertin, who was one of the forces that shaped the modern revival of the Olympics. Coubertin's original vision involved an equal celebration of sport, art, and culture. However, the IOC forum evolved into a celebration mainly of sport, with art and culture relegated to supplementary roles. Interestingly, the Olympic Arts Festival, held in Atlanta from June 1 to August 4, 1996, was reputedly the largest cultural event thus far.[34]

In an event that features men who wear as much makeup as women, and who are typically stereotyped as "effeminate," "gay," and "unmanly," there has been a persistent anxiety in rhetorically setting up competitive ballroom dance as a credible sport. The most common strategy, used particularly by advocates, has been the adoption of analogies to universally acknowledged television- and Olympic-worthy sports such as football or swimming. Nevertheless, this type of rhetoric flows spontaneously into a second rhetorical strategy: maintaining a tight balance between two persuasive thrusts by first pointing out the proximity between DanceSport and other canonical sports, but then also emphasizing their differences so as not to be caught in the bind of being judged by the standards of another sport. Thus, Christopher Hawkins and Hazel Newberry of England, winners of the 1997 World Championship, argue against a simplistic adoption of the Olympic motto of "*Citius, Altius, Fortius*—Faster, Higher, Stronger," in order to avoid the nightmare of "an Olympic gold medal being [automatically] awarded to dancers who in Quickstep can run *faster*, hop *higher*, or hold each other together *stronger* [devoid of artistic considerations]!"[35] Margaret Lonsdale, a former competitor who became instrumental in the evolution of ballroom dance in Australia, used her influence as executive director at the Western Region Sports Assembly in the mid-1980s to lobby for physical performance tests comparing ballroom dancing to other sports. She claims, "It was demonstrated that the fitness level of our dancers matched elite athletes."[36] A *Genesis* DanceSport Academy website reported that according to a 1986 study conducted by the University of Freiburg, the muscular exertion and breathing rates of DanceSport athletes performing a single dance number equaled the same body readings drawn from cyclists, swimmers, and an Olympic 800-meter runner over the same two-minute period.[37] The Canadian Amateur DanceSport Association chimed in, citing the same German study, and then continued with this remark: "Results showed that a DanceSport competition required all the same kinds and degrees of exertion and physical demands as running the 800-metre race. The only exception is that at major international championships, DanceSport competitors may be required to perform the same competition four to six times a day, sometimes for days in a row!"[38] A spokeswoman speaking on behalf of the Dancers Remedial Clinic in London chimes in, "Dancing is a really excellent way of keeping fit. It exercises most of the body. It keeps the joints mobile, works the heart and lungs, improves blood flow, shapes the muscles and generally makes you look and feel better." Even more significantly, the *New England Journal of Medicine* in 2003 reported that elderly people who danced frequently had a 76 percent lower chance of developing dementia because dancing improves memory as it involves having to remember steps and patterns of physical movement.[39] A promotional website for DanceSport trumpeted the following claims: "Dancesport is very physically demanding. Medical studies done at Oxford University in 1988 showed that 'championship ballroom dancers require a level of fitness equal to that of an Olympic decathlete in order to compete successfully.' "[40] That same study, according to this DanceSport promotional website, found that "the physical exertion level found in dancers following a two-minute Viennese Waltz was equal to the exertion level found in an Olympic track athlete completing the 100m hurdles."[41] The excerpt above about the Oxford study is strategically located beside a close-up photo of a woman in a Latin costume, her face lit by an enigmatic smile, accompanying the caption: "Making it look easy?"[42] The juxtaposition of image and text here is meant to highlight both how sporty DanceSport can be (that is, how much physical exertion it demands from its performers) and how it exceeds sport by aesthetically concealing effort, rather than nakedly displaying it.

The same website also describes the competitors in a ten-dance competition where the dancers perform five standard dances, such as the slow foxtrot, waltz, Viennese waltz, tango and quickstep, and five Latin dances, such as the cha-cha, samba, rumba, paso doble and jive. It compares the competitors to decathletes, who also strive to master skills for ten different track and field events. Yet, unlike decathletes, who benefit from their events being spread out over several days, DanceSport competitors must perform five of their dances in one session. Each dance lasts approximately at least two and a half minutes, with barely one minute of respite in between. Then, about two hours later, competitors must return, completely decked out in different costumes, in order to perform the other five dances. A 2002 article by William Porter of the *Denver Post* observes, "At the upper levels of ballroom dance, there is real exertion. It's athletic competition minus the grass stains. . . . Couples emerge from the floor breathing hard. This is the panting of winded athletes, not smitten lovebirds."[43] Stuart Nichols's outraged reply to Jonathan Bell's assertion that ballroom dance is not a sport because it does not allow for the drama of failure is well documented. He retorts acidly, "As one with 16 years full-time experience in the field, I can say with authority that there is ample opportunity for failure in DanceSport, drops, falls and injuries are very common. Were you to attend an actual event, or, better yet, attempt to train for and participate in one, I am sure you would have a different opinion."[44]

Peter Pover, former competitive ballroom dancer and past president of the U.S. DanceSport Council, takes the same aggressive stance: "In Germany, doctors did tests in which they wired up the country's 800-meter running champion and its amateur dance champions. They found no significant athletic difference between running 800 meters and doing the quickstep for $1^1/_2$ minutes. And that's just one dance. In competitions, couples have to do five 90-second dances in a row, with only 20 seconds between dances. Plus, the girls have to do it going backwards! All a runner has to do is jog around the track. And U.S. Olympic officials are patronizing about us?"[45]

Liz Murphy, administration manager of the International Dance Teachers Association, takes a more positive approach. Not only does she reiterate the health benefits of dancing, but she also plays up both the prestigious and social aspects of ballroom dance: "Dancing is now seen as a much more glamorous activity. I think its profile has been helped by stars like Ricky Martin, programmes like Fame Academy and films like Evita. . . . It combines your exercise class with a social night out. Because it all seems like a good laugh, then people seem more likely to keep it going."[46] Chris Malone, taking a similar tack, stresses its broadly based appeal from the 1920s to the 1960s and adds: "Even if someone is coming along just to enjoy the dance and the music, they find it relaxing and it takes the mind off the strains and stresses of what's going on during the day." In the rhetoric used by advocates, ballroom dance seems to be the perfect panacea to all ills, curing everything from bad posture and social awkwardness to poor self-image. Malone goes on enthusiastically, "If you begin to do reasonably in-depth work, then you start to work the posture, which improves your whole well-being. You walk taller and straighter, it can get rid of aches and pains in the back and makes people more confident." Appealing to the all-too-American obsession with losing fat, Malone throws his final sales pitch: "As far as calorie-burning goes it does depend on what level you're working at, but when you see professional ballroom dancers on the floor there's not an ounce of fat on them, so it definitely works."[47]

In addition to pointing out how much fitness and training DanceSport demands, its athletes also attest to its physicality and proneness to injury. "I've had black eyes, bloody noses, split lips,"[48] confides Michelle Officer, who, with her partner Edward Simon, are former U.S. champions. Brian Parkes, another competitor, scoffs, "I've had far more injuries in my three years of dancing than in the last 7 years of weight lifting. . . . I have sprained my left Achilles tendon, ruptured the right, developed Repetitive

Stress Injuries (RSI) in both my feet. I've pulled muscles in my back, fingers and calfs. . . . I've been assaulted by stiletto heels."[49] Other battle stories persist, such as that of a top amateur Latin competitor being kicked so forcefully that she was unable to compete for months, or of another woman whose thumb was broken by a sudden sweep from an adjoining couple's hand, or of "intentional collisions" that literally knock couples off their feet and can result in dangerous injuries.[50]

The analogy to other television-worthy sports is one heavily argued. Like football, DanceSport enthusiast Castillo Rangel argues, DanceSport inculcates "pride and heavy competition," with its resultant ranking system and promotion of community pride.[51] Both football and DanceSport are promoted, regulated, and perpetuated by governing bodies that recommend how athletes should prepare, how money should be divided, where arenas should be built, how exposure through the media should be promoted, and how competitive programs should be designed or modified.[52] Both football and DanceSport require their athletes to have speed, flexibility, and strength,[53] thus often necessitating that these competitors perform associated and preparatory exercises such as weight lifting, aerobics, stretching, and running. Both require appropriate physiques, with football linemen tending to be massive while ballroom dancers tend to be toned, thin, and well groomed. In both football and DanceSport, skill is a determinant in deciding how the athlete is to train. For example, if a football player can throw well and run long and fast, then there is a higher probability of the player's chances of becoming the team's quarterback. Similarly, DanceSport athletes may initially compete in several categories until they are certain of their forte and choose to specialize in that category. In both football and DanceSport, one must be not only physically agile but also mentally flexible, allowing for deviations from an original set plan in order better to adapt to changing circumstances of the play. In DanceSport, the ability to navigate a crowded floor with the contingencies of having other competitive couples performing around you, while continuing your routine, is called "floorcraft."

Both football and DanceSport require teamwork and an appropriate distribution of duties. The two activities have their own special equipment and uniforms: football players wear items like helmets and shoulder pads, while ballroom etiquette requires particular attires for particular dances. Typically, there are tuxedos for men and long, flowing gowns and shoulder extensions for women in the international standard or American smooth dances. Both football players and DanceSport performers have their own special shoes that are designed to aid their performances. And they have active spectators, who cheer on their favorites. Both also have their own mascots. In DanceSport, for example, Cardiff University carries the Welsh flag and numerous red dragon fluffy toys, two of which are nicknamed "Cha" and "Mambo."[54]

Yet unlike football, which relies on two opposing bodies colliding antagonistically against each other, ballroom relies on two bodies moving gracefully and seamlessly together, as if they were one body. Unlike football, which is male dominated and seems to leave no room for female participation (other than as cheerleaders), DanceSport requires a partnership between men and women, particularly at the higher levels. Although the man "leads" and the woman "follows," both partners are equally responsible for the performance to achieve its highest levels. While DanceSport enthusiasts might engage in fan behavior, particularly in cheering on their favorites, they differ from their football counterparts in that when they disagree with judges' decisions, they do not boo or hiss in reproach, but instead give standing ovations to their choices, while remaining polite and restrained when the judges' choices are announced.[55] This genteel reserve may be on the wane, though, with television producers encouraging their audience to shout nationalistic slogans like "USA! USA!"

Yet another rhetorical strategy emerges in the authorization of DanceSport as a sport, and that is the heavy use of scientific language. For example, in describing how ballroom dancers collaborate, John Derbyshire of the *National Review* writes, "Probably the best attribute a dancer can have ... is a keen intuitive grasp of Newtonian mechanics: how objects move in space under the action of forces."[56] Castillo Rangel goes overboard in the use of scientific jargon to validate DanceSport's sportiness, explaining here the relevance of cardiorespiratory endurance to success in ballroom: "Aerobic refers to oxygen requiring. . . . Testing may be theorized and practiced in various manners. In predicting maximal oxygen uptake, in a healthy athlete, strike volume increase of the heart due to training is studied. . . . The work intensity becomes your independent variable x, and any differences in heart rate or respirations results in the dependent variable, y. When the body becomes active it creates more ATP, a cellular unit of energy created in the mitochondria (the powerhouse) of the cell."[57]

Yet after such an elaborate (and obfuscating) use of physiological and biochemical terms, the only conclusion Rangel arrives at is that "measuring physical action(s) provides data to aid in proving the sportiveness of any sport." Corky Ballas, who shared with his wife, Shirley, the title of International DanceSport champions for the United Kingdom in the 1990s, is less oblique: "In peak performance my [resting] heart rate was 47 beats a minute. That's as good as any gold medallist. I look at people who can throw a javelin, run 100 metres—they might be able to skate all they want to, but let me see them cha cha cha. They can't do it, any of them."[58]

This rhetorical strategy of comparing DanceSport to other recognized sports breeds another subtype, which Ballas's earlier remarks illustrate:

that of debunking other Olympic sports using the very same criteria used by detractors to discredit DanceSport. Chris Dorst, vice chairman of the USOC's Athletes Advisory Council, had dismissively remarked, "If you can smoke and drink while you're actually competing, that's not a sport."[59] E. M. Swift, hardly able to contain his sarcasm, shoots back, "Hasn't he ever heard of yachting? That's an Olympic sport, but it's easier to light up and sail sloshed aboard a Flying Dutchman than it is to puff up and drink while doing the rumba. If Dorst insists on belittling disciplines he considers nonathletic, why not start with shooting, a so-called sport in which Olympians ideally have the heart rate of a cadaver? Or curling, Canada's answer to the shuffleboard?"[60]

The term "sport" is defined by *Webster's Ninth New Collegiate Dictionary*[61] and *Webster's Third New International Dictionary*[62] as: "any activity or experience that gives enjoyment or recreation; pastime; diversion; or "such an activity, especially when competitive, requiring more or less vigorous bodily exertion and carried on, sometimes as a profession, according to a traditional set of rules." Given such a loose characterization, it is hardly surprising that some DanceSport advocates strongly believe that DanceSport has more than fulfilled the requirements for being called a sport. Yet there are other considerations, such as the antidoping requirement,[63] necessary for eligibility for full Olympic sport status, and more recently, a consideration that has absolutely nothing to do with "sportiness"—its appeal for television audiences. Thus, Rudolf Baumann, president of IDSF, has boasted that in addition to providing a "dazzling spectacle," DanceSport is "guaranteed drug-free, with muscle build-up [the usual temptation for drug abuse in relation to Olympic sports] a no-no beneath the sequins and feathers."[64] In another publicity release he remarked, "We have 50 per cent participation of women. It's a clean sport. . . . We don't need new construction. We can compete in any hall. . . . We are the summer version of ice dance."[65]

The analogy to ice dance is a double-edged rhetorical blade. During the 1984 Winter Olympics, Jayne Torvill and Christopher Dean skated into first place with a competitive performance to Ravel's *Bolero*, awarded twelve "perfect 6" scores out of a possible maximum of 18. Ten years later, however, continuing with their groundbreaking moves, one of which was identified as a "lift," the result was that they were dropped to the bronze, apparently because they were perceived as making a sport event too arty.[66]

A discussion on this analogy within the IOC produced the following argument: "It looks like the difference between dancing and ice dancing is probably the ice. . . . Ice dancing presents an enhanced challenge simply because you wouldn't normally dance on ice. Both are definitely very interpretive and artistic. But it seems that the ice is what makes ice dancing a sport."[67]

Another charge against ice dancing is its propensity for subjective rather than objective judging standards. The debate pits DanceSport enthusiasts against each other, with Canadian Amateur DanceSport Association president Jim Fraser vehemently proclaiming, "The judging can be almost as objective as mathematics,"[68] while a successful amateur competitor like Soo-Mi Choe, who, with her husband, Charlie Hunter, captured the senior (age thirty-five and up) Latin and American category, remarked that judges often favor nonathletic qualities.[69] Mike Connolly, in an editorial, went as far as proposing that not only DanceSport, but any other "arty" sport like it be thrown out of the Olympics: "Lugers don't get [a] five second head start if their uniforms are a prettier color and ski jumpers don't get extra meters added to their jump if their eye shadow is nice. But somehow those things matter in figure skating [and DanceSport]. Choreography is great on Broadway but has no place in athletic competition."[70] Even Clive Phillips, a former champion who, with Suzanne Somers cohosted the first A & E televised broadcast of the 2001 Standard and Latin DanceSport Championships, remarked, "It's a subjective business at best; it is not a science." Nevertheless, in order to shore up DanceSport's status as a sport that can be judged, Phillips repeatedly fell back on one word, "commitment," stating that judges could assess which couples "best committed themselves" as they performed the basic movements of twisting, gesturing, turning, bending, weight transfer, and jumping (with stretching being added to the criteria for the Latin dances).[71] Interestingly, the USABDA's own, which has a brochure designed as a "Spectator's Guide to Amateur Dance Competition," acknowledges the subjectiveness built into the process of judging, but attempts to overcome that through an implicit appeal to the power of averaging out differences: "During the event, up to seven judges will rank the dance couples based on their skills, presentation, and showmanship. Scores from all the judges are combined to obtain the final standings. Adjudication is a subjective process (to say the least) and that is why several judges are used to ensure fairness."[72] Choe's and Phillips's remarks are not without basis. Even in South Africa, where couples often cannot afford dance lessons and often learn from videotaped lessons, the mishap of having a strap falling off the shoulder or an ill-fitting dress have proved sufficient grounds to losing the provincial finals. Bill Toseland, who has spent thirty-three years creating ballgowns, dance dresses, and wedding dresses, is emphatic in his support of the aesthetic (and commercial) elements of the sport: "No matter how dedicated or talented you are . . . your dress is as important as your performance."[73]

The emphasis on aesthetic appearance in relation to having a more effective overall impression contributes to stereotypes concerning the differences between typical sports and DanceSport. As K. C. Patrick points out, typically in American culture when one speaks of "elite athletes," the following adjectives are easily conjured: healthy, naturally talented, forcefully goal motivated, focused, lucky, and highly successful. Unfortunately, when one speaks of "elite dancers," different connotations are aroused, with "elitist" now meaning "undemocratic" and usually being used as a rhetorical mechanism to deny public funding or support.[74]

Patrick's comments make clear what is at stake in labeling DanceSport a "sport": the economic promise of corporate sponsorship, television coverage, and possible superstar status. Margaret Lonsdale, Australia's most vocal promoter of DanceSport, reveals that before the push to get ballroom certified as a sport, there had been earlier attempts to seek financial support under the arts banner. That failed, however, because the competitive nature of ballroom rendered it anomalous with the arts criteria.[75] Given that failure, it is hardly surprising that DanceSport's advocates expend a great deal of energy in making sure the label "sport" sticks: it spells the difference between an arcane hobby reserved for enthusiasts and a global multi-billion-dollar business.

Following is an analysis and summary of the main arguments the IDSF puts forth in order to sell DanceSport as a viable Olympic sport (and business):

1. The inclusion of DanceSport in the Summer Olympics will add to its appeal, as ice dancing has contributed to the appeal of the Winter Games (a problematic appeal, given the controversies surrounding the objectivity of ice dancing; but also an equally persuasive argument, in terms of garnering popular viewership as controversies add to a sport's mass coverage).

2. DanceSport already has such a popular base that inclusion would not require a significant increase in the number of athletes and officials.

3. DanceSport, unlike other sports, does not require major construction, as it can be performed in a wide range of already existing venues or arenas. Temporally, it will only take two days to complete the competition rounds, unlike other sports.

4. DanceSport not only has 100 percent gender parity, but it is also one of the few sports in which men and women athletes can simultaneously compete against each other on the same surface.

5. DanceSport attracts a huge international TV viewership, mostly female—something that most sports channels usually cannot reach

as easily. An eleven-year joint venture contract with IMG (1997–2008) ensures the worldwide TV distribution of DanceSport.

6. DanceSport adheres to the strict antidoping requirements characteristic of Olympic sports.

7. DanceSport is "nonaggressive" and "no violence has ever occurred amongst competitors or the audience"—a clear attempt to distance itself from the likes of the Harding-Kerrigan scandal in ice skating, or the attacks on athletes perpetrated by overzealous fans, such as in tennis, among other sports.[76]

8. DanceSport does not cause "extreme stress" on the human body, and thus does not cause "systematic injuries" to the body—a rhetorical claim that directly contradicts earlier testimonies stressing the physical expenditure necessary for maximum performance.

9. DanceSport integrates physical activity with musical expression and social interaction, and is invaluable as a basis for the physical and mental formation of young athletes.

10. It is highly democratic, accommodating all ages and abilities in appropriate ways, and does not require extra equipment or heavy expenditure for beginners.

[Note: This claim is based on a press release by the US Amateur Ballroom Dancing Association, and refers purely to the amateur circuit, as opposed to a professional-amateur studio arrangement.]

THE GLAMOUR AND THE BUSINESS OF DANCESPORT

On May 20, 1997, IDSF signed an eleven-year contract with Mark McCormack's IMG and its television company, TWI, furthering its reputation as one of the world's most successful and politically influential sports agencies. IMG/TWI engaged in some self-promotion by pointing out its successes in developing the marketing potential of various sports, including ice skating, golf, and tennis, and promised to use its forty years of experience and "imagination" to assist the IDSF in achieving its goals.[77]

Hardly surprisingly, to further authorize itself, IMG produced a star-studded list of clients and events, including athletes, federations, and international events. Some of the names dropped were Joe Montana, Chris Evert, Martina Navratilova, Andre Agassi, Pete Sampras, Dennis Conner, Monica Seles, Wayne Gretzky, Kristi Yamaguchi, Itzhak Perlman, John Madden, the Nobel Foundation and Harvard University, and the Wimbledon,

British, and United States Open Golf Championships.[78] The contract was dramatically unveiled at Planet Hollywood in Piccadilly Circus, London, where McCormack, serving as chairman, president, and chief executive officer of IMG declared, "DanceSport has the potential to become one of the jewels in the crown of the sporting world."[79]

The metaphors McCormack uses emphasize some of the very qualities to which DanceSport enthusiasts are ambivalently drawn, as with the promise of becoming "crown jewels" come the temptations of pandering to commercial interests, stripping the event of its aestheticism and spontaneity, and becoming shallowly glitzy. These tensions are particularly evident in the mechanics of holding the annual Blackpool Dance Festival at the Winter Garden Ballroom—still the most prestigious competitive ballroom event. Here, where traditions are tightly guarded, media passes for photographers and writers are actively discouraged and only three official photographers are permitted. All other interested photographers have to be seated as spectators and would have to shoot from whatever convenient location they could find, without any special accommodations being made for them. Although television cameras are permitted at Blackpool, they are there solely to record selected events on videotape; further, none of these videotaped materials is packaged for release to the networks.[80]

In contrast, in the summer of 1997, the U.S. Nostalgia cable television channel announced the beginning of its coverage of DanceSport. The year's Yankee Classic, a major competition held in Boston, was among the first of the events it covered. Immediately, the mise-en-scène changed: the ballroom was converted into a television studio, with a special backdrop being constructed for show dancing, so as to allow for "clean" shots (that is, devoid of spectators in the background); worse, this cut down the available room for a live audience by a quarter of its usual number. The Yankee Classic promoters added other extraneous features, such as the "Clash of the Continents" events, in which a team composed of U.S. dancers was pitted, couple against couple, against a European dance team in standard and Latin steps. The overall result seemed to render the term "floorcraft" obsolete (it takes no skill to navigate the floor when there is only one couple on the floor) and to threaten to replace "grace and elegance" with "glitz and glamour." Traditionalists' anxieties have been compounded by the fact that American smooth and rhythm styles are more flamboyant and seem tailor-made for television in ways that the international standard and Latin dances are not. As John Reynolds has written "When performing American Smooth steps, couples break from the closed position, often improvising their figures and literally revealing themselves to camera and audience. Women spin and twirl, raising the hems of their skirts in a manner that scandalizes traditional Standard dances, but tantalizes mass television audiences."[81]

For better or for worse, sponsors are beginning to line up: in September 2000, Timberline Ventures of Seattle made a $650,000 investment in DanceScape Corporation, the operator for the oldest online community for competitive ballroom dancing.[82]

Danskin sponsored the DanceSport Champions Series, an international competition of the top twelve professional dance couples, which was aired on New Year's Day, 2000, at 4:30 p.m. (Eastern Standard Time) on ESPN (November 24, 1999). The GoodLife TV Network created its own GTV DanceSport series, geared toward capturing "the artistic and athletic intensity, . . . the inside position into one of today's fastest growing sports" to its "thousands of fans."[83] Even Prince Albert of Monaco actively stumped for a World DanceSport Championship.[84] In addition, popular entertainers like Ricky Martin and movies like *Dance With Me* and *Shall We Dance?* have jumped on the ballroom bandwagon.

IMG has been ecstatic in its pronouncements regarding plans for publicizing DanceSport. A press release by Werner Braun, IDSF Press Commissioner, announcing plans to market the IDSF European Latin Championship in Innsbruck, Austria, staked out its virtual television borders like a conqueror demarcating his colonized territory. It boasted the following markets: Europe (Austria, Finland, Russia, France, Denmark, Spain, England), Asia (Japan, China, Thailand, Philippines, the Middle East), America (United States, Canada, Argentina) and Oceania (New Zealand).[85] Another later press release noted that during the broadcasting of the IDSF International DanceSport Championships, hosted by USABDA in Massachusetts, an initial rating of 5.0 had rocketed to 6.3 by the end of the show, averaging about 5.7 throughout the telecast. Braun enthusiastically claimed this as proof that "during the show excited viewers everywhere must have been telephoning friends and motivating them to turn on their TV sets or change channels."[86] The press commissioner estimated that the show was viewed by between ten and twenty million people in North America, and was pleased to report that DanceSport programs, based on this trial run, could compete successfully with well known TV hits like *Walker—Texas Ranger.*[87] In March 2000, *DanceSport Magazine* reported "high ratings" for the DanceSport Champions Series, which aired on January 1 on the TV sports channel ESPN. The program was an edited version of the Latin competition held at New York's Madison Square Garden in September of the previous year. The ratings suggested that DanceSport could command a viewership that could compete in popularity with mainstream sports. Even more significantly, the event has been billed as a "tune-up" for the Sydney Olympics, at which ballroom dancing was to be an exhibition event.[88] Amarilys

Valdes, president of DanceSport World Group LLC, enthusiastically remarked, "This is a new millennium and people are looking for changes in entertainment. Let's face it: Those dancers were hot and sexy, and a lot more entertaining than football. Anyone who watched would agree. We can't wait for DanceSport's Olympic debut and we are proud to have played a role."[89] Suzanne Carbone reported the choice of Melbourne as the site for the World Ten Dance Championship in December 2004, and credits the competition with "injecting $3 million into the Victorian economy."[90]

Despite the controversy swirling around whether or not to authorize DanceSport as an Olympic sport, one thing is clear: such an endorsement clearly would open the door to heavy commercial investment, and competition with other sports for funding within the Olympic infrastructure. E. M. Swift claims that USOC officials tend to get "testy" at the idea of dividing the money they have for nonrevenue sports. To counter this argument, Swift does a quick score sheet of mainly the economic benefits of authorizing DanceSport as an Olympic medalled event: "It's cheap, drug-free and politically correct, encouraging equal participation by both sexes. Facilities can be found everywhere, and the television ratings promise to be as strong as they are for figure skating."[91]

Despite the growing popularity of DanceSport and its successful forays into the realm of authorized commercialized sport, one area remains difficult to conquer: the gendering of ballroom as masculine enough to be considered properly "sporty." The roles of gender, alongside those of race, class, sexuality, and nationality, are the topic of the next chapter.

FIVE

Packaging Fantasy and Morality

GENDER, RACE, SEXUALITY, NATIONALITY, AND CLASS IN COMPETITIONS

Kathy Gibbons, national secretary of DanceSport South Africa, teaches ballroom at East Side College in Troyeville, Johannesburg, and in some other schools in the city. She laments the fact that there are no boys in these classes, blaming fathers who choose to encourage their sons to play soccer and rugby instead.[1]

Yet an interesting facet of ballroom, whether in the international standard, American smooth, or international Latin and American rhythm dances, is that gender, inscribed using a heterosexual (and an aristocratic class) stylus, are hyperbolically played out. Both the international standard and American smooth dances require that the men wear tails, vests, bow ties, and stiff plastic collars. In general, although men are allowed a certain amount of expressiveness when they dance—such as subtle, confident joy in the quick step and foxtrot, subdued delight in the waltz, and distanced satisfaction in the tango—men are usually expected to be stoic. Stoicism becomes aestheticized and conflated with the very essence of masculinity. In keeping with this conventional body rhetoric, ballroom dancing males tend to have a uniform look. Their function, in keeping with their assumed roles of gallantry and chivalry, is to frame their partner's more individualized and colorful costumes and moves (see fig. 5.1).

Women in the standard or smooth dances tend to have eye-catching and brightly colored gowns that are tailor-made to capture their movements. Their hair is elegantly coiffed, and they use shimmering jewels, stage makeup, and narrow-heeled, suede-soled pumps to complete the picture. Unlike the stern, distant, and controlled expressions of their partners, women are expected to display unbridled emotion that appears to verge on euphoria as they surrender themselves to their leads. Like those enacting aristocratic masculinity, the women embody and enact conventional notions of upper-class femininity in an exaggerated fashion, with ornamental display, emotional expressiveness, and surrender to male leadership.

Fig. 5.1 Note the upright military bearing with which the male lead frames his more ethereally clothed partner. *(Photo courtesy of Carson Zullinger)*

Thus, despite the glowing claim that "in DanceSport, women are equal with men,"[2] the aesthetic of DanceSport demands that the illusion of conventional gendered roles be played out. It is true that in competitive dancing, as opposed to informal club dancing, leading and following are not simply patterns of utter dominance and total submission, but despite this reality, for DanceSport to be seen as "beautiful," the appearance of women as decorative objects for their more stable and less colorful male partners is required—an embodiment of the idealized heterosexual paradigm.

It is common to hear feminists (especially those who do not dance) point out the patriarchal vocabulary and conventions of DanceSport that command that "men lead and women follow." Descriptions of dance figures are always visualized in terms of the lead's (man's) point of view, and men wear the numbers that identify the couples—leading some to point to the analogy of women assuming their husband's names when they get married. While all these are insightful, there are practical considerations that have to be kept in mind. In terms of costuming, for example, because of the often low or nonexistent back garments of the women, it would be difficult to tack on numbers there. Because international standard dances are done purely in closed position, never breaking away from that frame, women's gowns tend to be less flamboyant than their American smooth counterparts because their fronts tend to be concealed for the most part. To add an element of drama to their costumes, women who compete in this category often use boas, floats, or drapes around the shoulders to catch the judges' and spectators' eyes (see fig. 5.2).

Such accoutrements would be impediments to American smooth dancers because they tend to break away from and circle each other, rather than staying locked together. The roots of the American smooth style lie in the dancing styles developed by major U.S. studio franchises, such as Arthur Murray and Fred Astaire after World War II.[3] These studios, seeking to capitalize on the glamour of the Astaire-Rogers duo in popular movies, dropped the quick step and abandoned the closed position in favor of experimentation with open footwork, thus permitting the dancers to do steps side by side without touching each other, much like Latin dancers. Thus, American smooth gowns tend to rely on rich, deep colors, and eye-catching ornamentation, especially around the bodice. Their skirts are also often split up to the hip level to reveal the legs as the women spin, creating the hyperfeminized and colorful pictures that the hypermasculinized and more soberly dressed men frame (see fig. 5.3.)

Nevertheless, it is never a simple story: descriptions of the physique of particularly the Latin or rhythm female competitors vacillate across the hyperfeminized and the masculine. Journalist Alexandria Polier describes Ruola Giannopoulo's thighs as "small tree trunks" and claims that

Fig. 5.2 Women who compete in the international standard category often use boas, floats, or drapes around the shoulders to catch the judges' and spectators' eyes. *(Photo courtesy of Carson Zullinger)*

Fig. 5.3   The women are the hyperfeminized and colorful pictures that the hypermasculinized and more soberly dressed men frame. *(Photo courtesy of Carson Zullinger)*

Giannopoulo, a thirty-two-year-old Latin dancer originally from Greece, could be mistaken for a "professional body builder." Giannopoulo's descriptions of her workouts describe them more as a "grueling discipline" requiring dedicated work at not only practicing three to four hours daily, but also involving constant workouts at the gym to sculpt the body properly.[4] Once again, the characterization of the female (Latin) DanceSport body hangs in between eroticized and masculinized—either way, a spectacle of exotic otherness.

While the international standard or American smooth dances emphasize a European upper-class demeanor and dress, international Latin and American Rhythm dancers wear costumes that appear as glamorized equivalents to daily apparel worn in such places as the barrios of Havana, the streets of Rio, the bullfight arenas of Granada, or the nightclubs of Harlem. Here, gendered roles are displayed exaggeratedly, although sexual energy, flirtatiousness, passion, and even lust are openly displayed rather than sublimated, as in the standard or smooth dances. Men often choose blousy shirts, which are unbuttoned to navel length so as to display rippling pectorals, and they wear trousers that flatten the stomach and sculpt the buttocks. While male Latin or rhythm dancers are allowed flashier colors than their standard or smooth counterparts, an unwritten rule requires that they wear colors that do not overshadow their female counterparts. Women, though, are allowed even more latitude, choosing whatever shimmering, tight fitting, and skimpy outfits might enhance their sensuous bodily movements and reveal as much as possible of their well-sculpted physiques (See fig. 5.4).

In smooth or standard dances, an aristocratic look prevails such that women are expected to have their long hair styled to keep it firmly fixed yet in a style both dramatic and sophisticated while men are expected to have a short, conservative haircut with a clean line at the nape. Latin or rhythm dances allow women to have hairstyles ranging from chic short hair to ponytails, and men are allowed to cultivate whatever facial hair they want, even wearing ponytails or shoulder-length tresses. This is a case where long hair is part of the look of being hypermasculinized, precisely because it is racialized as Latin. Gendered, classed, and raced stereotyping, imbricated in intricate and naturalized ways, are therefore intrinsic to the look of these dances. Thus, Latin or rhythm dancers actively cultivate a bronzed look, part of the aesthetic of this type of dancing. Visits to tanning salons or numerous applications of self-tanning chemical solutions that make it appear that the competitors have spent a month doing nothing but sunning themselves at a Jamaican beach are part of the preparation for the

Fig. 5.4   An example of the form-fitting and sensual attire characteristic of Latin or rhythm dancers. *(Photo courtesy of Carson Zullinger)*

competition. In a parallel argument, Juliet McMains calls this cultivation of the Latin look "putting on brownface"—an act of costuming the white body to simulate the exoticism and hypersexuality associated with the stereotype of the Latin type. McMains sees this as a contemporary version of blackface minstrelsy, popular from the 1830s to the 1930s in the United States, which involved primarily Irish immigrants darkening their skin in order to perform gross caricatures of African Americans.[5] The assumption of artificially darkened skin ironically ends up obscuring the African American and Latin roots of these dances because DanceSport, in its evolution through the innovations of English, European, and American dancers, has increasingly grown further from its roots.[6] In contrast, there is no overt attempt at actively altering the skin color of competitors in the standard or smooth dances, since the women's costumes often favor a light pastel, ethereal look. Standard or smooth dances are often shot using a soft focus lens to aestheticize paler, dreamier hues; it is understood that European styled whiteness here constitutes the unspoken racial aesthetic.

Richard Dyer points out that whiteness is associated with power, heterosexuality, virtue, cleanliness, godliness, wealth, ethereality (if female), and universality.[7] Standard and smooth dances enshrine these racial and moral evaluations of European aristocratic whiteness while appearing to stand in as transhistorical and natural human values. He is ever chivalrous and dignified; she, always beautiful and transcendentally light. The privileged aesthetic principles emphasize vertical movement, the seeming effortlessness and lightness of body weight in fleeing from gravity, the flowing movement created by an emphasis on extended lines.

If the standard and smooth categories enshrine whiteness, then the Latin and rhythm divisions ambivalently glorify its racialized exotic Other, and it is important to note that the two types of competitions form a binary opposition—one needs the other in order to mark its place within the overall system. DanceSport's narrative concerning what is authentically Latin reveals more about Western fantasies than about what is ethnically or racially genuine about being Latin—in itself a contested category because of its homogenization of a diverse range of Latin American nations (as well as a diverse range of skin colors, including white, black, brown, and innumerable shades of mestizoness). If standard and smooth dancing elevate the body in vertical lines, the emphasis in Latin and rhythm dances is on working into the floor, using gravity to express raw power, and sinuous but sharp hip movements to express hyperenhanced sexuality. The racializing of the female Latin competitor's body as Other on one hand allows her more latitude because there is a greater range of positions and motions she is allowed. Occasionally, she is even allowed to stand over her male counterpart (see fig. 5.5), unlike in the standard dances, where she remains pressed

Fig. 5.5   The racializing of the female Latin competitor's body as Other on one hand allows her more latitude; occasionally, she is even allowed to stand over her male counterpart. *(Photo courtesy of Carson Zullinger)*

against the man's side in a perpetual embrace. Yet the price of such freedom is high: though Latin movements enable greater innovation and creativity, these movements are also coded as less refined, or more primitive. Nevertheless, as Richard Dyer[8] points out, one may appropriate Otherness without giving up implied class and racial privileges; that is, artificially colored white skin is still recognized as white. Latin Dancesport is still ultimately white because it is a ballroom dance (and thus still emphasizes frame, balance, and control), as opposed to salsa, tango, and samba club dancing, where the creativity, spontaneity, rhythmic qualities, and freedom of Latin dancing are even more pronounced.

Abigail Feder-Kane's[9] comparisons of the media constructions of overdetermined masculinity and femininity in the men's versus the ladies figure skating competitions are instructive in characterizing representations of gendered interactions in DanceSport. She has remarked that the ladies figure skating competition's narrative motifs revolve around the repeated use of "soft focus lights, stars in little girls' eyes, glittering costumes, and flowers from adoring crowds."[10] Both Suzanne Somers and Clive Phillips engaged in similar rhetorical strategies in describing the dynamics of the 2001 Standard DanceSport Championships. During the Viennese Waltz segment, Somers remarked, as the camera used the soft focus, "I love the way the dress sails across the floor. It's what you dream of when you're a little girl."[11] Phillips continued in the same vein, "It's a fairy tale," remarking that the use of wings on the women's sleeves enabled the illusion of flight or flow.[12] Regarding the difference between the ladies' and men's heel heights, Phillips added that this type of heel enhanced the ladies' action; yet he didn't remark on how men, too, wear heels, even if they are significantly lower and do not have the spiked look of the women's shoes. Somers breezily added, "That's why we put up with it [wearing heels] all these years"—implying that the artistic exaggerations demanded by the dance overlap in a simple way with the everyday realities of what looking beautiful or graceful demand. In addition, the rapidly cut sequences to signal the transition to a commercial break, implying a peek behind the scenes of the competition, predominantly featured women rather than men, but principally in passive, more hystericized, and narcissistic poses. Backstage, a man stretched while a woman sat, dabbing her face delicately with a towel so as not to ruin her makeup. Another woman, shot in a profiled close-up, sat fanning herself, and in another montage, a woman cleaned her shoes, a couple practiced a few steps in closed position, and a woman paced, doing neck rolls to relax herself. While a man stood, a woman massaged her legs vigorously and nervously. Even during the times when the couples were not competing, they were shot as if these gendered roles naturally blended into the "real" world of backstage preparations.

One other similarity that Feder-Kane notes is summarized thus: "In figure skating, despite the similarity in skills performed, certain poses and gestures are gendered female. The most obvious is the forward layback spin. . . . Back arched, eyes closed, mouth slightly open, arms extended as for an embrace—in still photographs it looks nothing so much as popular conceptions of female sexual climax."[13] The description strikingly converges with a waltz move called the "oversway," which is often shot from the perspective of a high angle or a profile shot, looking down at or sideways on a woman as she arches her back in an exaggerated pose, her face bearing a look of exultation in surrender to the man's lead (see fig. 5.6).

Unlike the standard competition, which was predominantly shot using dissolves that emphasized smoothness and flow, the Latin competition was more like a men's figure skating championship, shot principally using rapid cuts that seemed to glow, as if to emphasize the pulsating energy of the dance. Whereas the women's standard gowns gave the illusion of simulated nudity (much like the lady skaters' costumes), such as through very low backs, the women's Latin costumes were unabashedly sexual. Still, despite the overt display of power and athleticism through its use of dips and drops, as in the coverage of the standard dances and ladies figure skating, the athletes were never shown grunting, panting, or sweating (see fig. 5.7). The

Fig. 5.6 Note the exaggeratedly arched back of the female competitor as she is supported in a version of an oversway by her male lead. *(Photo courtesy of Carson Zullinger)*

Fig. 5.7 Note the seeming effortlessness of the athletic pose. *(Photo courtesy of Carson Zullinger)*

men, too, were heavily sexualized, running the risk of becoming eroticized objects of the gaze. In her commentary on the jive finals of the A & E 2001 Latin DanceSport Championships Somers remarked on the Italian dancer, Riccardo Cocchi, "Speaking of behind, I think he's got a great behind."[14] Phillips, her cohost, was unable to think of a rejoinder.

McMains points out that the masculinities of, in particular, the male Latin dancers are constantly under siege. Male Latin dancers straddle the positions of being hypermasculinized (and thus run the risk of being characterized as brutish or sexist) as well as effeminate (because of their exaggerated hip motions and stylized gestures).[15] Along a parallel track, Marta Savigliano[16] analyzes tango lyrics and concludes that Latin men who dance the tango disrupt conventional gendered roles by being forcefully dominant and even violent in their assumption of the macho aesthetic while being feminized by their undying passion and search for genuine, lasting love. Basing her conclusions on her own experiences as a professional competitor in the Latin dances, McMains claims that "nearly half the professional male Latin competitors in America are openly gay."[17] This oxymoronic confluence of traditional heterosexual masculine ideals (such as strength, power, decisiveness, and rugged gallantry characteristic of "real" men, usually from a lower class) and nontraditional male homosexual traits (such as flamboyance, self-spectacularization, and the attention to the minutest detail of aesthetics) potentially opens up new avenues through which one could negotiate, expand, and reinscribe the boundaries of masculinity. Unfortunately, that is not what has happened. Instead, both the racialized and sexualized stereotypes of the Latino dancer remain fully in force. As McMains claims, "But such realignments do little to actually promote an open acceptance of homosexual identity since there is no gay male couple represented in DanceSport performance. Even if gay men find a space to resolve tensions at a personal level, they must still perform a public persona of heterosexual man in a romantic relationship with a woman."[18]

Interestingly, one way in which the male dancers' masculinity was protected during the 2001 competition was by portraying them, as any other male athlete, as excessively competitive and driven to win. While his partner, Oksana Nikiforova, stood silently beside him, the German Franco Formica, boldly declared, "We will not give anyone anything for free."[19] Similarly, Andrej Skufca, who together with his partner, Katarina Venturini, had won the British Open in an unexpected upset over Russia's Dmitriy Tumokhin and Anna Bezikova, coolly remarked, "We deserved it. We knew exactly what [had] happened."[20]

Just like an Olympic event, nationalistic rhetoric was also part of the competitive framing, despite protests from Christopher Hawkins and Hazel Newberry, highly successful World Amateur Champions in 1997, that they "do not really believe there is a 'National' style of dancing" and that there are only individual couples, who happen to come from different countries.[21] During an interview featured at the 2001 DanceSport Competitions, the leading standard DanceSport couple from England, Jonathan Crossley and Kylie Jones, were asked to reflect on any changes they had used in order to win. Crossley began to mention how, despite their success in England, their results were not as high when they competed internationally, particularly compared with the Italians. In one of the few gender-role ruptures, his partner broke in and hastily added, "We did not want to lose the English style of dancing, but you can't win with just one style."[22] In addition, despite the fact that none of the U.S. competitors won, their making it to the finals or semifinals was always framed as a triumph and as an indication of future success to come. Thus, when Victor Fung and Eve Pauksena took sixth place in the standard competitions, the commentators remarked that they must be "very proud" especially as they had been competing for only one year together; when Eugene Katsevman and Maria Manusova, Eastern European émigrés who had become American citizens, were unable to advance to the finals, Phillips and Somers remarked that they were "very young" and therefore would have more opportunities in the future to win the top slot.[23] Similarly, in their review of the quarterfinals of the Latin DanceSport competitions, the commentators framed the U.S. couple Kevin King and Olga Rodionova's entry into the quarterfinals as a "surprise" triumph, and the dynamic performance of the leading U.S. couple, Eugene Katsevman and Maria Manusova, in the jive as a straight ticket into the semifinals. In contrast, an Italian brother and sister (Stefano and Annalisa de Filippo) team's failure to advance onward (a fact that was also true of King and Rodionova) was rhetorically framed as a disappointment. Similarly, the Italian couple Riccardo Cocchi and Joanne Wilkinson's winning of the fifth spot in the Latin DanceSport Championships was described as a "step back," despite their win over the U.S. couple, who had ranked seventh. Finally, as if to ease some anxiety that all of the top U.S. couples had foreign origins (Fung was Chinese American; Pauksena's country of origin was not mentioned, but she had a distinct Eastern European accent; Katsevman and Manusova were both Ukrainian, moving to the United States in the 1990s), Katsevman and Manusova, the leading American couple who came away with seventh place overall, were given a long write-up that featured how American they felt, especially in the aftermath of the events of 9/11.

The rhetoric surrounding the "Russian invasion" of American ballroom dance is likewise refractory. For example, Joseph Berger's article "The Russians are Coming, Stepping Lightly" moves in between the dangers of an alien invasion and the tantalizing heritage of continuing Fred Astaire's unparalleled dance career.[24] The "Brothers Atanasov—Dmitre, Vladimir and Alex" are identified as exotic (note how the way in which they are introduced makes the trio sound like Dostoyevski's *The Brothers Karamazov*—which would be mysterious and alluring to an American audience) but also as Americans-in-the-making. Berger's use of quantitative data drums in the point of the sheer numbers of immigrants flooding the U.S. market for Dancesport: "In New York, New Jersey and Connecticut, immigrants from the former Soviet Union now own 11 of the 23 Fred Astaire dance studios, the chain of franchises Astaire founded in 1947. And there are an additional hundred or so Russians who teach in the 89 other Astaire studios around the country."[25] Yet Berger is careful not to render the Russians and Eastern Europeans as too exotic. Their grace, panache, and precision, in his description of them, are a continuous link from Astaire's day, and their athleticism and energy have expanded the frontiers of ballroom dance experimentation in the United States Berger provides an explanation for why these immigrants often outstrip their American youth counterparts. He claims they were "born to dance."[26] In the tradition of the great czarist balls, Russian youth begin lessons as early as the first grade and continue at least until the fourth grade. Furthermore, the Soviet Union set up rigorous dance programs for the most promising youth in order to garner as many international awards as possible, and thus gain international prominence for their native motherland. Ballroom dancing, according to Berger, became both a sign of culture in Russian society, as well as a surrogate for the spiritual vacuum left by the banning of the practice of religion. Berger concludes his article on an optimistic note: he domesticates these Eastern European interlopers by casting them as students of capitalism, or more precisely, Americans-in-the-making.

> But they are learning some of their capitalist skills from Americans. "We're learning how to run business, how to be successful, how to make dance studio a hot spot," Mr. Tarsinov said. "We Russians don't know how to sell and we like to learn."[27]

The tensions in the quotation above are evident. Mr. Tarsinov is the ultimate example of the American dream: the promise that anyone, with hard work and an intelligent assimilation of core capitalist values, can prosper in this environment, which is ostensibly free from racial or ethnic prejudice. Yet the careful use of the quotation above, with its omission of articles, serves to mark Tarsinov's speech patterns as a non-native English speaker even as it proclaims his success. The article claims to interpret the influx of Russian ballroom teachers into the United States as a revenge against or reversal of the ending to the 1957 hit musical *Silk Stockings*, in which Fred Astaire uses flashy footwork and a kiss to convert a long-legged Ninotchka, played by Cyd Charisse, to the joys of capitalism: "Now, in real life in the United States, the Russians seem to have turned the tables, wielding their elegant footwork to take over the art Mr. Astaire is most identified with, and doing so in true capitalist style," writes Berger.[28] Nevertheless, there is a sense in which such a Russian victory is pyrrhic: the true winner is capitalism—which is, given the rhetorical backdrop, ultimately and quintessentially American.

These many rhetorical points of tension reveal that like other sports, DanceSport is already negotiating how to package its gendered, racialized, sexualized, nationalized, and classed dimensions so as to encourage commercial appeal, using the narrative frame of the competitive melodrama to heighten audience interest. In that sense, it has already made the transition into being an Olympic sport.

SELLING A DREAM: ADVERTISING DANCESPORT

McMains conjectures that the exaggerated stress on the "brown-ness" of DanceSport's Latin competitors is a mechanism through which the real issues are kept concealed. She points out that though what DanceSport sells is the image of glamour, its economic structure, based on the pro-am system, is rooted in the economic dependency of its teachers on their students. Professionals, despite their glitzy exteriors, usually do not have as much economic stability as their students, and are parasitic on their students in order to finance the mounting costs of outfits, coaching lessons, and constant traveling and competing: "Most professional dancesport competitors in America finance their expensive coaching and travel schedules by selling their services in pro-am competitions. . . . Dancesport professionals . . . usually have little college education or significant earning potential outside the industry. Most come from working-class backgrounds, many of them recent immigrants. . . . No one wants to admit that Latin dancesport professionals hail from the lower classes if they are also masters of its classy movement technique."[29]

McMains makes the argument that "under a guise of ethnographic representation of third-world dance forms, movement that might otherwise be read as low-class in the American context can be transformed into high-class art."[30] In other ways, the exaggerated stress on race masks the real source of anxiety: the license to enjoy an erotic display in which nudity and the sexual act are unabashedly represented as properly aesthetic and high class, while exorcising the spectacle of its formal costuming and narrative similarities akin to those characteristic of strip clubs and escort services. Brownface racializes class anxieties, or displaces and masks these anxieties concerning class differentials onto racially marked bodies.

McMains's argument is certainly convincing, as being part of ballroom activities is certainly prestigious. The very costs of the gowns, shoes, hairdo and makeup, lessons, competitions, and travel expenses are immediately prohibitive. Only those belonging to a certain class, and who can therefore afford the leisure of these expensive, aristocratic activities, are part of this private club of DanceSport practitioners. Yet there is a sense in which class is also very overtly so much a part of the packaging of the glamour being sold that it cannot be seen as a stable hidden term. Rather, I think it is more important to map the dynamic relationships binding race, class, gender, sexuality, and nationality as intersectional, rather than privileging one term: class. To make class the master term (that is, the term that determines the mechanics of raced, gendered, sexualized, and nationalized discourses) is to oversimplify extremely complicated processes. I will illustrate what I mean through an analysis of several ads, which are selected, not quantitatively or mechanically, but for the complexity in their composition, which renders more visible what is often glibly brushed aside in some of the other ads.

An interesting example is the ad for the "Sole Saver Shoe Brush."[31] It begins with a quotation from Nietzsche, wrenched completely out of context: " We should consider every day lost in which we do not Dance at least once." The fact that Nietzsche meant "dance" as a oneness with the realm of nature, as opposed to the world of culture (of which ballroom dance, with its hyperbolic emotions and poses is a penultimate illustration) is of no consequence. It is clear that the target market for the product is an educated audience—or at least one schooled enough, or aspiring to be sufficiently literate, to recognize Nietzsche as a philosophical and literary figure. Interestingly, the term "sole saver" is so close to "soul saver" that one cannot help but catch the echoes of the clever pun—and its implied promise of salvation from the perils of dirty, unkempt, slippery shoes.

The ad continues, "If you'd like to clean the soles of your shoes, safely and in style, then you have come to the right place." At face value, the ad is simply advertising a brush to maintain the condition of the suede on the bottom of ballroom shoes. Yet the metaphors embedded in the ad conjure a "home" of "cleanliness," "safety" and "style"—all of which are correspondent with the fantasy of the ideal ballroom dancers as moral, upwardly mobile, and classy role models. The lines are accompanied by an abstract drawing of a man and woman dancing cheek to cheek, in an Argentine-tango-style embrace, with the woman's buttocks showing slightly from a slitted dress raised by her right leg that is draped seductively over the man's left leg, as he caresses her leg with his hand. The drawing, despite its abstraction, seethes with the steamy eroticism of its Argentinian bordello beginnings, but the accompanying text that redefines its consumption obscures that. The "Sole Saver," now continuing with the thinly disguised church metaphor, offers "peace of mind" because "it comes with its own attractive case" and therefore can be inserted into a pocket, purse, or shoe bag—resulting in a clever rhetorical conjunction of convenience (a secular value) with "peace of mind" (a nonsecular one). The drawing also "whitens" the illustration's Latin roots, and renders "natural" its implied heterosexuality. But the ultimate punchlines are reserved for last: Not only is it "handsomely designed" (an adverb that transforms the gender-neutral brush into a masculine escort, though one could also presumably, in old-fashioned locution, refer to a woman as "handsome") to "belong" (and to authorize its owners) in the ballroom cosmos of "glitz and glamour"; more importantly, the brush was designed by Marcia Halpern and Bernard Matos, amateur ballroom dancers. The use of the term "amateur" is important, as it labels its designers as being of the common populace (as opposed to ethereal professionals), and yet also as competitors whose names can be recognized. The juxtaposition makes the implicit claim that Halpern and Matos, through their successful experiences, know what real ballroom dancers need: "It was designed by ballroom dancers *for* ballroom dancers."

The full page spread for J'ordy, a company that sells custom-made original costumes and ready-to-wear practice clothing for men and women, is equally intriguing. The photo, by Gary Brown, displays two prominent female DanceSport champions, Diana McDonald and Elena Grinenko, identified in text underneath their gracefully posed feet, apparently emerging from dark curtains, as mirror images of each other. Both ladies have one of their hands appearing to hold the curtains against their bare shoulders and barely concealed breasts (a gesture that hovers in between modesty and coquettishness); each woman also has one elegantly sandaled leg protruding from the dark curtains, angled flatteringly in a typical "Betty Boop" pose that is characteristic of Latin and rhythm dances. Both women have the "come hither" look typical of archetypical seductresses, and Diana McDonald's blonde, All-American, mature look complements Elena Grinenko's dark-haired, exotic, more youthful appearance. "What are They Wearing?" is the question the ad, on the surface, poses, but the real question it asks (for potential female customers) is: "Would you like to be as beautiful, glamorous, successful, and mysterious as they are?" (That is, would you like to be as privileged, white, heterosexual, essentially all-American as they are?) Its answer: To be as they are, wear J'ordy, a name that evokes resonances with French couture. Interestingly, the ad, which aligns itself with the artistic tradition of the female nude, also markets itself for the potential male patron and promises the equivalent heterosexual fantasy: the possession of women of this type, and the prestige and power that accompanies such possession. After all, the ad unabasedly sells "gowns, suits, dresses, dreams"—with the preponderance of products geared toward women, thus revealing its main target audience.

Though there are ads geared toward both men and women, most of the ads seem to be directed principally at women. For example, dancenaturals-usa.com, a company that carries different brands of ballroom shoes (whose names and contact information are listed in small print at the right side of the ad), has a large, diaphanous lady's shoe, suspended and superimposed, in a manner similar to a Magritte painting, over the façade of a stately Italian building, whose arches allow light to flood over most of the area occupied by the shoe. The rest of the composition is balanced by the darker elements on the right, implying the transition to an interior, complete with multiple images of candles sitting atop a chandelier-like candle holder. Minus the large shoe, the photo is very much reminiscent of some of Magritte's visual puns, where interiors and exteriors loop into each other. Other than the clear attempt to sell the shoes as works of art, the implication is that because the shoes are made from genuine Italian leather, they share in the cosmopolitanism and rich cultural heritage of Italy; purchasing these shoes seems to imply acquiring an exotic and elegant pseudocitizenship of Italy. The makers of the ad could have chosen both a man's shoe and a lady's shoe to be the principal motifs, but that is not the case. It is clear whom they consider their principal audience.

When men do appear in advertisements, they are never alone and clear objects of the gaze, the way women are. Even when their bodies are fragmented, the way women's bodies are, their (heterosexual) masculinities are never compromised. For example, another full-page spread for the Can-Am DanceSport Gala (the Canadian Open Professional Championships) in 2003 shows only a couple's legs, high above the evening skyline of Toronto, the site of the event. While the man has dark trousers and black dance shoes that cover every part of his body, the woman's legs are bare, save for the glittery hint of stockings and fringes, with her feet enclosed in the usual delicate two- or three-inch heeled ballroom shoe. It is clear who the center of gravity is: the man's legs are planted firmly with one foot slightly pointed to the side while the (invisible) torso faces squarely to the front; the lady's legs are slightly angled, with a toe on the back foot angled slightly outward, showing the immediacy of her openness and responsiveness.

Interestingly, even abstract representations preserve the same dynamic. DancingArt.com sells a broad variety of art items for the "dance enthusiast," including active wear, gifts, greeting cards, and logo designs, among others. To the right side of the ad, in an orblike structure, are the outlines of a man and a woman dancing. While the outline of the man's frame is clearly identifiable (it is clear where the head, torso, and legs are), the woman's frame is less clear, save as curvaceous, flowing lines that drape themselves around the solid outline of the man. It is only after one has stared at the ad for a while that one realizes what the lady's position is: she is flung over in an oversway, barely supported by the man's hand. Unlike the man, whose legs are clearly outlined, her legs are a graceful but confusing blur. DancingArt.com claims to sell "emotion, imagination, reality"—implying that artistic representation (which is differentially gendered, classed, sexualized, racialized, and nationalized) merges with reality,—and thus de facto promotes a certain view of the ideal ballroom archetypes.

A catalogue displaying Lynn Wallander's designs is one of the very few ads that feature a black woman prominently. The African American woman occupies the center foreground, looking directly and unabashedly at the camera, with her right arm provocatively on her right buttock and her left hand gracefully poised atop her left thigh. Her hair, though it bears traces of some kinkiness, is tightly tied up in an elegant hairstyle—an effect that whitens her look to some extent. Nevertheless, it is important that she remains in the role of the sexy primitive relative to the two other white women behind her. Though it is the African American woman who occupies the center stage, her body stance reflects sexual aggressiveness and availability more overtly than the two others who occupy the background; she also wears the flimsiest outfit, cascading with glittering rhinestones and palettes. Behind the African American woman, at midground and to the first woman's right, is a blonde woman with her hair similarly pulled up in a tightly composed coiffure. Her arms are similarly draped behind her back, resting on the shape of her buttocks; however, she is posed more demurely than the African American woman, with her eyes averted in a serious expression and her legs posed such that her thighs remain closed. Her dress, though one appropriate for a Latin or rhythm competition, does not reveal as much as the one in the foreground does. The third woman, in the background, to the African American woman's left, is a white full-figured woman wearing a standard gown composed of a dark and a light color, split vertically by shiny material. Her hair is dark and appears to be braided atop her head. She, too, looks modestly away, though she smiles even as she arches her back and uses her left hand to raise one tip of her skirt. Her inclusion in the ad is a clear message that women with less than perfect bodies, too, can aspire to some measure of elegance and beauty. Unlike the other two, who are frozen in statuesque poses, this woman appears spontaneous and natural, and it is important to note that she alone wears a smile, making her seem even more natural than her beautifully posed companions. Her appeal lies in her humanity, while the appeal of the other two lies in their mythic qualities as primitive sex goddess and blonde unreachable fantasy object.

These ideal forms are also enshrined in film, advertisements, and artifacts of popular culture in general, which are infused with global capitalist values, as we have seen. The last chapter of this book constitutes an exploration of alternative paths to the Olympic dream.

SIX

Quo Vadis?

In chapters 4 and 5, tracing the evolution of ballroom dance from a recreation or performance art into a competitive sport has served as a test case through which rhetorical constructions of gender, race, class, sexuality, and nationality may be critically examined. The point of the exercise has been less to bash this highly popular and demanding art and sport form than to point out the ambivalences and complexities that studying, practicing, competing in, performing, and teaching DanceSport entail. Admittedly, ballroom choreography at this point predominantly privileges a heterosexist, patriarchal, white, aristocratic aesthetic. Nevertheless, there have been experimental breaks from the system; they neither have become widespread, nor do they constitute all-out revolutions against the status quo, but they reflect a yearning for something different. It would thus be wise to close this book with an examination of a few noteworthy instances of a critique of DanceSport's raced, gendered, classed and sexualized aesthetic.

DANCESPORT COMPETITIONS

In Dancesport competitions, a new category called "showdance" has been initiated, which allows a couple to perform a solo choreographed piece to music of their own choice for three minutes. Dima and Olga Sukachov's 1999 Ohio Star Ball showdance rumba was a particularly bold experiment. Though their number still entailed traces of conventional costuming (she wore a very tight, short-skirted black outfit and high heels; he wore a black bodysuit), it was clearly an attempt to revisualize the conventional narrative of the rumba. Using techno music, characterized by a slow, even beat, the couple walked slowly in, in time to the music, their hands at their sides. For the majority of the number, they performed the same steps side by side, with their hands quietly at their sides, quite unlike the typical hyperactivity of the hands characteristic of Latin dancing, with their exaggerated display of curvy feminine lines and straight masculine lines. When they did use their arms, which was well into their number, they used very simple figures: the cucaracha, a side-to-side motion; the alemana, a basic turn; a rope spin; rumba walks which reversed, such that at times it seemed that they took turns leading, with him moving forward in one sequence, only sharply reversed, with her advancing toward him the next. There were no dips or drops or splits, which have come to be part of the standard spectacle, and which tend to perform the masculine/feminine dichotomy of domination/submission. In addition, though the couple's costuming did entail traditional elements, it is important to note that she was not swathed in the usual extra rhinestones or glitter so vital to demarcating the female in conventional ballroom presentations; instead, her hair, like his, was simply tied back, as if to create an androgynous look. He, as well, did not have the usual chest-revealing top characteristic of most testosterone-inspired male Latin costumes. The fact that both of them wore serious expressions, rather than the typical flirtatious or coy facial expressions for her, and the typical powerful, domineering expressions for him, further enhanced the androgynous look: none of the usual sounds created by Latin dancers as they simulate sex were in evidence. Everything about the routine was clean, quiet, and precise. The quietness of their movements forced the camera, so used to miming the conventional dance's hyperactive movements and assuming a voyeuristic stance to shoot them predominantly in side-by-side medium or long shots, drawing attention to the unadorned synchronicity of their movements, executed in stark simplicity.

Ron Montez, one of the Ohio Star Ball's hosts, and former Latin champion, exclaimed in surprise that he had never seen the rumba portrayed this way before. Sandy Duncan, the other host, described it as "very new millennium" and declared that she liked it. Montez, the seasoned competitor, carefully remained quiet on whether or not the rumba reinterpretation was pleasing to him. Unfortunately, the Sukachov's inventiveness was not valued by the judges that year; they ended up sixth—the last place in the finals. Bill Sparks and Kimberly Mitchell, who performed a conventional paso doble, done admittedly with tremendous energy and attitude, won first place, which tells us how entrenched the conventional expectations are.

While the Sukachov's dance experiment could be hailed as a radical break away from particularly traditional characterizations of gender, substituting a more equal androgynous relationship between the two partners, there are dangers that lurk in their interpretation. One problem is that there is a possibility of interpreting "androgyny" as absolute sameness, which is plagued by the tyranny of utter homogenization. One could argue that because their costuming differentiated them as male and female, there is no obliteration of sex, or that there is a natural flow from their sexes to their genders, which are subtly played out. While these are decidedly welcome innovations, one wonders whether the unchanging quality of their expressions, which could be described by detractors as mechanical, is any better than the inflated hyperexpressiveness so characteristic of standard ballroom competitions. And the idea that sex and gender can be conflated, where male bodies "naturally" produce masculine lines and female bodies "spontaneously" generate feminine lines, ends up ironically reifying the heterosexist hegemony.

One could argue that the simplicity of the Sukachov's costuming was a critique of the conventional class and racial depictions of competitive Latin dancing, with its oxymoronic combination of higher class privilege with raw, sexual primitivism. Yet if critique means the complete obliteration of differences—the radical leveling to utter sameness—then that alternative is also problematic. Nevertheless, the audacity and difference of the Sukachov's presentation must be acknowledged and given its proper due, particularly as compared with the other showdance numbers, which pandered to the conventional expectations.

There are other numbers that ironically end up strengthening the very gendered binary dichotomy they seek to critique. Kenny and Marion Welsh performed alongside Stephen and Lindsey Hillier in an exhibition titled Tango Magic at the 1993 Ohio Star Ball. The four dancers each transformed themselves into a simulacrum of a couple, with each person having male and female parts: the idealized metaphor of "one body with four legs," used by the tango maestro in Saura's *Tango*, became dangerously literalized. On the lower halves of their bodies, they enacted the circus trick of gendering the two halves by a vertical split. They donned pants and flat shoes on their left legs (since men always lead with the left), and their right legs were each adorned by hose, a satin pump, and a skirt. Regardless of whether the performer was actually male or not, the performer's head was gendered as masculine, and to represent the woman, a puppet's head was used. The end result was that the woman's role in this number was essentially reduced to that of being a leg and a painted puppet's head. The choreography reinforced this idea as most of their steps were done from the male lead's perspective. Occasionally they performed more feminized gestures, such as kicks, rondes, and attitudes, but these were clearly more the exception than the rule. Ironically, even as they attempted to deconstruct the idealized and commercialized archetype, they reified it and showed how absolutely necessary two bodies are (or at least two sets of legs—with the woman's head and torso somehow being rendered inessential) in order to attain the speed and power typical of DanceSport performances. While one could argue that the experiment showed that both men and women can lead with equal dexterity, it is important to note that they all effectively enshrined the masculine role as the indispensable one, and thus remained rooted in conventional depictions of gender and power. Though their fictional bodies were bisexual, even these metaphorically paired bodies remained heterosexual, in keeping with the mores of DanceSport. There was no evidence that the raced and classed dimensions of ballroom dance were even touched. Nevertheless, the effort at reconceptualizing should be noted and applauded.

Another experiment in problematizing gender conventions occurred in Bill Sparks and Kimberly Mitchell's 1998 Ohio Star Ball performance. She, wearing a revealing bright yellow outfit, typical of Latin competitions, strutted in, bearing with her a chain and a collar, in which the imprisoned Bill Sparks, wearing a standard black bodysuit, was ostensibly trapped. Their initial theme song was Elvis Presley's "You're Nothing But a Hound Dog," which humorously set the context for why he panted like a dog and begged for the privilege of dancing with her. After playing the dominatrix to the amused crowd for a short while, Kimberle settled into a conventional Latin routine. Once the routine was over, she once again took up the chain and led the apparently dominated Bill off the floor, accompanied by amused hoots and laughter from the audience. Unfortunately, despite the highly entertaining nature of the dance, the simple reversal of power relations does nothing to deconstruct conventional gender modes, particularly if the performance is framed as a joke, in order not to emasculate the male dancer too much. Ultimately, traditional depictions of race, sexuality, and class remained intact in this routine.

Another more successful routine, also using humor, was performed by Nick Cotton and Maria Hansen at the November 1997 Ohio Star Ball. This waltz, choreographed by Wendy Johnson and Michael Babineau, centered on the humorous attempts of the quintessential gentleman (Cotton) to get rid of a tenacious bit of toilet paper that sticks to various body parts (his shoe, his hand, his partner's back, his partner's hair) as he attempts to romance the quintessential lady (Hansen). The structure of humor may be explained via Arthur Koestler's notion of the continuum binding the "haha" experience (comedy) and the "aha" instance (artistic creation and scientific discovery). Briefly sketched, the psychological mechanics of comedy are essentially the same as other creative acts: these functionally entail the sudden clash between two mutually exclusive codes of rules, or associative contexts, which are suddenly juxtaposed. What results is "bisociation"—a condition that compels us to interpret the situation in "two self-consistent but incompatible frames of reference at the same time; it makes us function simultaneously on two different wave-lengths."[1] (The frisson caused by bisociation is purged through either laughter, scientific fusion, or artistic confrontation. As Koestler writes, "The conscious or unconscious processes underlying creativity are essentially combinatorial activities—the bringing together of previously separate ideas of knowledge and experience. The scientist's purpose is to achieve *synthesis*; the artist aims at a *juxtaposition* of the familiar and the eternal; the humorist's game is to contrive a *collision*.[2]

Koestler's description of humor is particularly apt as the crux of Cotton and Hansen's routine hinges on the juxtaposition of several normally separated planes: the very polite, formal clothing and elegant steps of the waltz alongside the crude incongruity of a piece of toilet paper within that setting; the man's frenzied attempts consciously and repeatedly to dislodge the offending article alongside the woman's (apparent) blissful obliviousness to the (apparent) concealment of his frenzy; and the use of a scatological object (usually used in a private space) in a DanceSport competition (a hyperexposed public space). The joke is complicated as it is initially not clear what is feigned and what is real. A few moments pass before the spectators realize that the toilet paper is supposed to be stuck on Cotton's shoe and is not an inadvertent faux pas. With that comes the recognition that it was the audience that was initially duped by the joke, and laughter follows. The audience can then indulge in the illusion that they know more than Hansen, who now becomes the duped and the butt of the joke. Yet the audience is also hyperaware that this is a carefully choreographed routine, as evidenced in her impeccable timing in making sure her line of vision uncannily just misses the location of that offending article numerous times, prolonging the suspense and humor of whether or not she will eventually spot it.

Part of the reason why the audience easily forgives Cotton for making them the initial butt of the joke is that they empathize with Cotton's all-too-human situation, and recognize one of their deepest anxieties as DanceSport performers: the possibility of being in a similarly embarrassing situation, such as when one's zipper is inadvertently left open, or one's dress accidentally falls down. Hansen's unperturbed look of blissful romance even as the audience laughs loudly highlights a central absurdity experienced by many DanceSport performers: projecting the illusion of an archetypal emotion (such as romance, passion, or sexual desire) while feeling a very different set of private perturbations (fear, anxiety, anger).

The crux of this multifaceted joke is that Cotton projects two contradictory identities simultaneously. On one hand, he is the stuff of fantasy: the ever-gallant and suave gentleman who knows how to charm and show off his lady. On the other hand, he is also a comedian, whose clumsiness seems at odds with his other glamorous persona. For the illusion to work, the gentleman has first to fool the audience, and then to fool the audience into thinking that he is fooling her. Similarly, the lady's corollary role is first to make it appear that he is fooling her, and second, to fool the audience into thinking she is the one being fooled. The conscious enactment of what is usually repressed opens the possibility of being self-reflexive about the gender roles stereotypically represented in DanceSport exhibitions. Though the humor is lighthearted, it pokes fun at the typical role playing DanceSport performances usually demand, and creates the possibility of finding issue with the stereotypes of the perfect gentleman and lady that the commercialization of DanceSport egregiously promotes. As such, the joke is not simply a release of tension resulting from the juxtaposition of two usually incompatible frames—it also has a potentially subversive, reconstructive dimension. By making the parody more ironically appealing and entertaining than its earnest, glamorized ideal, the joke offers an alternative to the typical constructions of gender and power in DanceSport competitions.

This experimental routine is one of the few that managed to garner public recognition. It was awarded the first place that year, winning the hearts of both the judges and the audience. Nevertheless, even if the routine was successful in problematizing traditional characterizations of gender and power, it failed to address concrete and intersecting issues dealing with race, class, and sexuality.

STAGE PRODUCTIONS AND FILMS

There are two movies that I have discussed in chapter 3 that are noteworthy in relation to critiquing DanceSport's conventional ideals. These are *Strictly Ballroom* (1992) and *Tango* (1998).

Because I have discussed the rhetorical dynamics involved in *Strictly Ballroom*'s representations in detail in chapter 3, I will simply limit myself to succinct points in this chapter. *Strictly Ballroom*'s genesis seems to lie in a revenge story. According to Ray Rivers, an Australian DanceSport champion who competed in the 1960s, the film's origins were formed by the narrative of a former ballet dancer turned ballroom competitor whose innovations in competitions were consistently snubbed by the judges. Irrespective of the creativity, skill, or popularity of his choreography, his radical breaks from the standard choreographical canons went unrewarded. Rivers claims that every time he beat this man, the loser vowed, "This is rigged! I'm going to make a movie." And indeed, thirty years later, *Strictly Ballroom* becomes a landmark film in contemporary representations of DanceSport.[3] Given the context of the movie's putative origins, it is hardly surprising that the film is rife with parody. The movie's humor relies a great deal on hyperbole, and the supreme manifestation of that exaggeration is Mrs. Hastings, who has been described as a "magnificent dragon lady, with her industrial strength perm, ozone-alert tan, and a body-hugging leotard whose garish design is best described as psychedelic vomit."[4] Yet humor has an effective edge only when the difference between the parody and reality is paper thin; it is not an accident that the film blurs the documentary mode with the melodramatic but generally lighthearted musical. As Ebert perceptively remarks, "The true weirdness of the movie comes when we begin to realize the director didn't make everything up; only real life could possibly have inspired a world this bizarre."[5] As we have seen in earlier chapters, the drive to transform ballroom dance into DanceSport has striking affinities with this comically dark universe, with its emphasis on competitive spectacle, hyperenhanced glamour, and commercial appeal. And given the movie's rootedness in a revenge story, it is hardly surprising that there is nothing redeeming about the way in which the DanceSport industry is represented. Precisely because the film's diegetic alternatives to conventional representations of gender, race, class, and sexuality hinge on a simplistic dichotomy between the ballroom industry's "fake" staging and an interracial couple's "genuine" expression, its diegetic alternatives are ultimately as conventional as the problems it critiques. Its radical outlining of the problems that plague DanceSport, both as a mode of representation and as a set of institutionalized practices (for example, the de facto restriction of creativity, the judging system's openness to corruption, the "whitening" of Latin dances; and the constant cover-up of the darker sides of the industry in favor of a glamorous fairy tale that performers and spectators have a stake in upholding) is therefore weakened by its equally problematic appeal to the stock ugly duckling-Cinderella fairy tale and the romantic narrative of the rebel overcoming the establishment by sheer force of genius and charisma. Purely as a diegetic, the film's gains in reconstructing conventional modes of representation are ambiguous. However, as an act of recreation—or of restaging DanceSport conventions for reaching out to a wider public audience, *Strictly Ballroom* is decidedly a step forward.

Tango's experiments in tango choreography are similarly striking, and there are two scenes that I wish to focus on. Since I have done a detailed plot description and analysis of this film in chapter 3, I will move straight into an examination of these two specific dance sequences. In the first, Suarez, the director–narrator, aims the "windmaker," an enormous fan, at a delicate array of women's dresses. The dresses flutter and then dissolve into the interior of a women's dressing room. Then, in a fantasy scape, we see Elena, dressed in a delicate white flapper's costume, dancing a tango with the more androgynously and darkly attired Laura. It is Laura who leads Elena in a lesbian interpretation of the tango, culminating in an ardent mouth to mouth kiss as other female couples look on seductively and approvingly. The gender dynamics of the dance would have been revolutionary had it not been clear that it was staged by Mario for his own viewing pleasure. As Geoffrey Macnab remarks, Suarez "is, for all of his grace and humour, intensely voyeuristic. When we see Elena, his beautiful new discovery, dancing with . . . Laura, we're in no doubt about his mixed feelings of lust, anger and jealousy."[6] In addition, though two female bodies are shown, they are clearly demarcated as fulfilling feminized and masculinized roles still very much in keeping with a heterosexual paradigm. That is, Elena, dressed in delicate white, plays the role of the follower and is clearly the pursued; Laura, dressed provocatively in dramatic black, enacts the role of the leader and is obviously the pursuer. Shortly thereafter, Elena returns to Mario to declare her abandonment of Larocca in favor of accepting his offer of living with her, reinscribing the patriarchal frame of the narrative.

The second scene initially resembles a nightmarish fantasy scape created by Mario's fevered mind. It later turns out to be a preview for the producers, who strongly suggest that the material be excised from the show. Here, male soldiers march in as Elena, wearing a peasant's dress and looking rumpled and vulnerable, looks distressed. She runs as various characters weave in and out, depicting various types of torture, with all the torturers sexed as male and all the victims sexed as female. The explanation for the insertion of this scene comes through a voiceover which explains that during the military regime (initiated by the infamous 1976 coup) that resulted in numerous disappearances, tangos were played loudly in torture rooms in order to drown out the screams of appeal, pain, and protest. The use of the tango as both an aid to the "art" of torture as well as its critique is brilliant, but devoid of social and historical context, the sequence hangs in a vacuum. Furthermore, its inscription of conventional modes of gender and power (with the tortured as female and the torturers as male) undercuts its revolutionary potential as a means of reconfiguring the possibilities of not only the dance, but also the genre of the musical. Ultimately, the dance sequences in general, arresting as they may be, tend to fetishize particularly the women's bodies. For example, in the tango triad, which enacts the rivalry between two women (Laura and Elena) over one man (Laura's dance partner and possible new paramour), in order to signal her bid for attention, Laura does powerful multiple turns. Instead of catching her whole body, inclusive of her determinedly expressive face, the camera instead rapidly cuts to a close up of her skirt, which flies up teasingly, both hinting at and denying the view of her crotch. Though the film ends up emphatically upholding the conventional racial and classed characterizations of the tango (that is, it upholds the aesthetic of the exotic, primitively passionate Argentinean, dressed in the most luxuriously beautiful attire), the film is worth noting for its attempts to expand the expressive and narrative range of the tango.

Tango, as mentioned in chapter 3, is a film about making a stage production, and a film about making a film. *Burn the Floor* (2000) is a film about an international traveling stage production, bringing together forty-six champion Latin and ballroom dancers from fourteen countries. This movie version of the show was filmed at its world premiere in London. The production clearly markets itself as aligned with popular contemporary ballroom films as the back cover of its DVD takes a blurb from *USA Today* declaring the film to be "Strictly Ballroom with Attitude." Yet it also aligns itself with Hollywood cinematic conventions through its use of some more traditional numbers, such as "Cheek to Cheek," a foxtrot with a clear reference to Astaire and Rogers (ironically down to Rogers's feathered outfit that Astaire reputedly thought an instance of severely poor taste)[7] and "Top Hat, White Tie and Tails," whose music is derived from an Astaire-Rogers number in *Top Hat*, yet whose costuming and choreographic group formations (particularly as revealed by an overhead camera) are very reminiscent of Busby Berkeley's work. It also aligns itself with the commercially successful *RiverDance*, yet attempts to add narrative as a clear component of the dance production. As one critic remarks, "*Burn The Floor* is not exactly a play, and even though music is vital to the production, this isn't really a musical in the typical sense. Instead of using dialogue or singing to tell the story, the performers use dancing to convey the message, which is basically how dance has evolved and the different styles that exist."[8]

What is potentially revolutionary about this set of performances is that it attempts to create an eclectic mix of ballroom, modern, jazz, Lindy Hop, jitterbug, and Latin dancing. Frederic and Mary Ann Brussat enthusiastically catalogue the array of dances and scenery changes: "The program features dances including the waltz, cha cha cha, samba, rumba, jitterbug, salsa, tango, Lindy Hop, jive, and swing. Let these dancers transport you to a masked Viennese ball, a Spanish bullfight, or a World War II jitterbug celebration."[9] Two dance sequences in particular illustrate this revolutionary potential.

"Urban Heat" is the best representative of how this production pushes the usual dance genre boundaries. The inspiration of this number comes from the desire to mesh standard ballroom and Latin dance with urban and industrial dance. The narrative context appears to be derived from *West Side Story*, which is in turn a modern American adaptation of the essential plot of *Romeo and Juliet*. Here, the two teams representing either the Jets and the Sharks (if using the *West Side Story* template), or the Montagues and the Capulets (if resorting to the *Romeo and Juliet* narrative frame) stride forcefully onto the floor amidst resounding metallic beats. Both "gangs" wear the same type of cyber-punk costumes and don dreadlocks (looking as though they have just stepped out of a *Mad Max* movie), but are demarcated from each other purely by a swath of color adorning their clothing: bright orange for one group and neon green for the other. The women wear tight-fitting, small-skirted leather costumes; the men wear equally tight-fitting leather tops and pants. Both wear a lot of chains. The collective number involves group numbers in which the two gangs compete against each other, as well as a solo in which a lead couple, using predominantly rumba steps, lustily emote the act of coupling—an act which is clearly tabooed by both groups as they endeavor to separate the couple, who waver between seeking out and fleeing from the other.

In terms of gender representations, the number is noteworthy because its hip hop sections enable the women to be freed temporarily from the follower position and to execute the same steps alongside the men, displaying power and strength. When they fall into more conventional choreographic patterns, such as dips, the women do not have the look of wonder-filled abandon they are required to display during ballroom competitions, but an entire gamut of emotions, including lust, anger, fierce competitive delight, and combativeness. Different types of partnering systems are allowed, enabling women to dance with women and men to dance with men, in addition to the usual male-female pairing. However, it is important to note that even these unusual pairings are marked as heterosexual by virtue of their exaggeratedly combative and fairly fleeting nature within the context of the duration of the entire fifteen-minute sequence. The men, while being freed from the requirement of being militarily stoic, do not deviate far from the stereotype of maschismo required by Latin dancing.

The general costuming is radically set against the aesthetic of ballroom, where even when primitivity is valorized (as in the Latin dances), glamour is an essential component in their costuming. Instead, both men and women wear very stark black and white makeup, set in patterns on their faces and bodies in a way that simulates tribal markings in an antiaesthetic. Modernism and primitivism hang in a tight balance. It is still a fashion statement, of course, and these are probably no less expensive than the conventional ballroom costumes, but it is an attempt to work against the stereotypical representation of glamour (and class) in the usual ballroom performances.

However, the use of dreadlocks and facial makeup give the number not only a primitivistic look, but also a decidedly African aesthetic, even if all of its performers are white. Thus, the number cannot resist the cultural advantages that the act of performing brownface, as McMains calls it, bestows on its practitioners.

The camera work is probably what inspired the comparison to *Strictly Ballroom*. It is also frenzied and manic, matching the high energy of the music and the dancers' movements, which have been described as "lively, energetic, even frantic."[10] The producer of the show, Harley Medcalf, described it as "the theatrical version of Viagra," and indeed the majority of the numbers and the way in which the show is shot are characterized by a nervous stream of energy. The camera work cuts rapidly from long shots to medium shots to close-ups of various body parts and then returns to long shots and even overhead shots (to show the group formations on the elevated stage), occasionally interspersing reaction shots, revealing how the crowd is responding to the performance and how those within the performance simulate the act of spectating. Occasionally, a slow motion is inserted, depicting the sweat flowing from the dancers' bodies, and there is a slight tear between the pacing of the music and the imagery shown. Fred Astaire's austere and elegant style of shooting has clearly lost to Baz Luhrmann's spectacle-oriented camera work, but minus Luhrmann's parodic hyperbolizations.

Both men and women are featured voyeuristically through shots in close-ups that move up and down their bodies. As a critic delightedly observes, "There are a lot of hot looking dancers (of both sexes, for those interested) in varying shades of undress in this show. Lavish costumes that would be at home in any Broadway musical get stripped down to bathing suit sized ones in the middle of numbers."[11]

At first glance, this seems to imply a greater egalitarianism. Unfortunately, that is deceiving. The men, when they are eroticized, are often shot at a medium range with their upper torsos bare, their rippling muscles glistening with sweat; this still allows the viewer access to their extremely expressive faces. The women are more typically given the tight close-up of the crotch or especially the buttocks, particularly when the buttocks are barely harnessed by lacy material or brightly colored thonglike underwear; these shots are devoid of faces, unlike the men's.

The second number, titled "The Passionata," seems a cross between Bizet's *Carmen*, as evidenced in its use of music from that opera, and *Camelot*, the quintessential tale of a love triangle, as evidenced by the knightlike insignia that sit atop the two male dancers' armorlike tops. The class registers of this dance are already instantly muddled: the story of an unrepentantly seductive prostitute is integrated with the story of a chaste, aristocratic woman who turns to the convent when she fails to keep her marriage vows. Opera, an art of problematic status, is combined with a legend about royalty and dancing that is considered decidedly upper class (ballroom). In terms of dances, the number combines the paso doble, the ballroom dance depicting the interactions between the bullfighter (male) and the cape or bull (the female), the Argentinian tango, and modern elements of dance. The choice of the paso doble in itself allows the woman to explore more complex realms of femininity than that of conventional delighted abandonment as she can either be a teasing cape that enables the bullfighter to exert his power, or an angry bull that could gore the man. The costuming of the main female dancer is particularly noteworthy: the camera focuses on a large African-looking headdress underneath which artificial red hair spills, topped by purple horns. These become visible as the woman slowly undresses, stripping a gauzy red cape and a long, brightly colored grass skirt and black bodice to reveal sexy black stockings, a tight-fitting top, and a very tiny red skirt.

The woman initially appears to be a conventional muse as she travels between the two men, causing them to stop and gaze at her and follow her movements in order competitively to display their masculinities to her via their cape-twirling skills. (Interestingly, Fred Astaire does a similar maneuver with his coat in a balcony scene with Audrey Hepburn in *Funny Face* [1957]; however, while the two men in *Burn the Floor* do it in competition with each other, Astaire performs in order to appease Hepburn's irritation at his meddling in her night life in Paris.) Indeed, the trailing gauziness of her costume at this point makes it seem as though she were disembodied, floating across the floor.

Yet later, when she has stripped down, revealing that magnificent body, it is she who initiates dancing with the two men, playing them against each other. The tension escalates as the woman alternates dancing with each of the men until one of them forcefully takes her and imprisons her with his arms. He violently takes her extended arm that is reaching out to the other lover downward, implying his triumph over her will as a silken red fabric runs over their bodies, signifying the closure of the narrative. This number is ultimately more conventional than the first number: it preserves the look of exotic primitivism characteristic of Latin dances, and it is fiercely heterosexual in its configurations, even in its group sequences. Nevertheless, it does blur, to some extent, the conventional boundaries separating "high art" and "low art," and allows the female dancer, to some extent, a greater range to initiate movement, and for a time, direct it. The sequence does end in the woman's death or subjugation, as happens in *Carmen*; nevertheless, insofar as it raises the specter or threat of a completely independent female sexual choice within a clearly patriarchal narrative, it makes it noteworthy.

The point of this chapter is not to show that there have been no gains in breaking away from conventional modes of glamorizing ballroom; neither is it to show that such gains are ultimately impossible. Rather, the crux has been to show that there have been various attempts made to destabilize the value systems built into current practices of ballroom, and that these attempts represent ambiguous gains. The critical and balanced analysis of these rhetorical constructions, enacted through bodies and other texts, should therefore be perceived as a call, invitation, and exhortation to continue explorations of how representations of gender, race, class, sexuality, and nationality may escape the mold, while being familiar enough to be accepted by not only the DanceSport community, but also by the larger public.

It is important to note that in the documentary bonus section of the DVD of *Burn the Floor*, the act of working on this production is contrasted several times with the act of competing. Though many of the participants knew each other from competitions that pitted them against each other, they had not formed any camaraderie. They were simply disparate couples— all very gifted, but used to being uncaring about anything more than themselves outperforming everyone else on the floor at the same time. Both the director and several participants repeatedly spoke of the effort it took to establish the necessary rapport for this motley group of ballroom stars to function as a dance troupe. Yet they also all spoke of the emotional rewards that a spirit of cooperation, rather than competition, bestowed upon all of them. And this would not have been possible save for the type of funding this endeavor was lucky enough to acquire; such a mechanism of economic support clearly aligns it more with an "arty" tradition rather than a "sporty" context.

The insight is useful, as it returns us to the point at which we began. Is DanceSport better served when treated as an art or a sport? Should ballroom evolve completely into DanceSport and eliminate its social forms, in pursuit of media prominence, and with that, greater financial resources? How realistic would it be to propose that the march to achieve Olympic status as a medaled sport be abandoned in favor of more artistic alterna- tives, given how competitive and relatively meager the resources are for the arts, as opposed to sports? Ultimately, I think enabling a balance of different types of funding mechanisms would be the most productive answer; thus, the conservative thrusts of competitive (sporty) ballroom could be maintained alongside the more radical experimental choreography enabled by treating it as an art. Perhaps, as well, it is not so much that ballroom needs to be reenvisaged completely as DanceSport, but that the notion of the Olympics needs to be returned to one of its earlier interpretations, in which sports, aligned with the values of a patriarchal, heterosexual, white, privileged com- munity, do not have such a hegemonic prominence over the arts.

Ballroom-Dance-Related Organizations

(Cited in Chapter 3)

CANADIAN AMATEUR DANCESPORT ASSOCIATION

Based in Switzerland and representing nearly 9 million DanceSport competitors worldwide, the Canadian Amateur DanceSport Association is one of 78 NSF members of the International DanceSport Federation (IDSF).

Website: http://www.dancesport.ca/

Address:
Canadian Amateur DanceSport Association, 200–4603 Kingsway, Burnaby, B.C., Canada V5H 4M4
Phone: (604) 433-0010
Fax: (604) 435-0269
E-mail: president@dancesport.ca

DANCESPORT WORLD GROUP, LLC

The DanceSport Champions Series is the concept of DanceSport World Group, LLC, the business leaders in the DanceSport industry, which is the exclusive representative of the DanceSport Championships Limited tour (the largest tour of Pro-Am, amateur, and professional grassroots competitions) and agent to DanceSport athletes and talent.

Relevant Websites:

Press Release:
http://www.prnewswire.co.uk/cgi/news/release?id=42319

News Article:
http://www.findarticles.com/p/articles/mi_m1083/is_3_74/ai_59870972

Article (includes pictures):
http://www.justsalsa.com/newyork/dance/contest/dancesport/9-18-99/

INTERNATIONAL DANCESPORT FEDERATION (IDSF)

The IDSF is the only continental federation for DanceSport. The website provides access to different committees, events, Olympic information, statues, and rules along with other information.

Website: www.idsf.net

Address: International DanceSport Federation, Avenue Mon Repos 24, C.P. 83, CH 1000 Lausanne 5, Switzerland
Phone: (41 21) 310 47 47
Fax: (41 21) 310 47 60
E-mail: generalsecretary@idsf.net
        cfreitag@ibsnet.info

INTERNATIONAL DANCE TEACHERS ASSOCIATION (IDTA)

The IDTA provides the public and professional performers as well as teaching devices with examination services. The association uses modern technology to keep up with growing trends to provide the most efficient examination service. The IDTA is a government-accredited QCA body and works with other government agencies to keep up with growing trends that have an influence on dance.

Website: www.idta.co.uk

Address: International House, 76 Bennett Rd., Brighton East Sussex BN2 5JL, England
Phone: 44 (0)1273 685652
Fax: 44 (0)1273 674388
E-mail: info@idta.co.uk

INTERNATIONAL MANAGEMENT GROUP (IMG) AND TRANS WORLD INTERNATIONAL (TWI)

IMG is an international sports management group and TWI is its affiliate television company. TWI was established in the 1980s and is the largest independent producer and distributor of sports programming.

IMG website:
www.imgworld.com
TWI website: http://members.fortunecity.com/teamfx2000/index/t

INTERNATIONAL OLYMPIC COMMITTEE (IOC)

Website:http://www.olympic.org/uk/organisation/if/fi_uk.asp?Id_federation=43

This website gives information about the International DanceSport Federation as well as information about Olympic committees and events. It links to the IDSF website.

UNITED STATES BALLROOM DANCERS ASSOCIATION (USABDA)

As the United States National Governing Body for amateur ballroom dancing and the competitive version of ballroom dancing known as DanceSport, which conducts activities under the trade name and registered service mark "USA DanceSport," the USABDA is a nationwide nonprofit organization of volunteers. Its aim is to inform and motivate dancers and educate the general public about the purpose, talent, and achievement behind this activity.

Website: http://www.usabda.org/

Address: Central Office, PO Box 152988, Cape Coral FL 33915-2988
Phone: (800) 447-9047
FAX: (239) 573-0946

UNITED STATES DANCESPORT COUNCIL (USDSC)

A registered trademark and division of the USABDA, the USDSC is responsible for regulating amateur athletes and competitions, in addition to coordinating all DanceSport activities in the United States, such as national championships.

Website: http://www.usabda.org/

Address: USA DanceSport, P.O. Box 128, Freedom, PA 17349
Phone: (800) 447-9047
E-mail: usabdacent@aol.com

UNITED STATES OLYMPIC COMMITTEE (USOC)

Tasked with representing and preparing America's athletes, coaches, and administrators of Olympic sport who go on to represent the United States in the Olympic Games, the USOC is an organization mandated by Congress under the Amateur Sports Act of 1978 to govern Olympic and Pan American Game activities in the United States.

Website: http://usocpressbox.org/

Address: United States Olympic Committee, One Olympic Plaza, Colorado Springs, CO 80909-5760
Tel: (719) 632-5551
Fax: (719) 578-4654

WORLD DANCE & DANCE SPORT COUNCIL (WD&DSC)

The WD&DSC is a group of twenty-two professionals from twelve different countries who comprise the leading authority on professional dance throughout the world.

Website: http://www.wddsc.com

Address: Company Secretary, Stuart Saunders, World Dance & Dance Sport Council Ltd
WDDSC Centre, Karolina St. 20, 28195 Bremen, Germany
Telephone: 49 421 13162
Fax: 49 421 14942
E-mail: secretary@wddsc.org
Registered Address: 7-8 Albert Road, Silvertown, London, E16 2DW, England

Appendix

Filmography of Selected
DanceSport and Ballroom Films

In addition to the major films reviewed in depth in the text, the following films are related to ballroom dancing and DanceSport.

Burn the Floor

United States, 2000
Dance
97 minutes; Dolby; color; English
Universal; MCA
Producers: Harley Medcalf, Maria Medcalf
Available from amazon.com

FILM FACTS

Directors: David Mallet, Anthony van Laast
Editor: Nick Morris
Choreography: Anthony Van Laast
Cast: Fergus Logan (Master of Ceremonies)

Story: *Burn the Floor* is a video of Las Vegas–style dance performances. The dancers use ballroom dance, modern, swing, and some ballet and are wonderful to watch. This film is filled with fabulous costumes, great lighting and stage design, and lavish dance performances.

Reviews:

Beierle, Aaron. CurrentFilm.com. http://www.rottentomatoes.com/click/movie-1094642/reviews.php?critic=all&sortby=default&page=1&rid=220247 (accessed March 31, 2004).

Brussat, Frederic, and Mary Ann Brussart. *Spirituality & Health*. http://www.rottentomatoes.com/click/movie-1094642/reviews.php?critic=all&sortby=default&page=1&rid=294174 (accessed March 31, 2004).

Campbell, Karen. "Dancers Cut Loose in *Burn the Floor*." *Christian Science Monitor,* March 31, 2000. http://search.csmonitor.com/durable/2000/03/31/p19s1.htm (accessed March 31, 2004).

DeWolfe, Cheryl. *Apollo Guide*. http://www.rottentomatoes.com/click/movie-1094642/reviews.php?critic=all&sortby=default&page=1&rid=189203 (accessed March 31, 2004).

Hines, Williams P. "*Burn the Floor* Sizzles." *SpotsSlights*. June 2000. http://www.homohome.net/spots/2000-06/articles/spots_lights-2000_06.htm (accessed March 31, 2004).

Short, Judge Norma. DVDverdict.com. April 6, 2000. http://www.rottentomatoes.com/click/movie-1094642/reviews.php?critic=all&sortby=default&page=1&rid=198006 (accessed March 31, 2004).

Wheadon, Carrie. Reel.com. http://www.rottentomatoes.com/click/movie-1094642/reviews.php?critic=all&sortby=default&page=2&rid=189205 (accessed March 31, 2004).

Dirty Dancing

United States, 1987
Dance/drama/romance
105 minutes; Dolby; color; English
Vestron Pictures; Great American Films Ltd Partnership
Executive producers: Mitchell Cannold, Steven Reuther
Producers: Linda Gottlieb, Eleanor Bergstein
Coproducer: Eleanor Bergstein
Associate producer: Doro Bachrach
Available from amazon.com

FILM FACTS

Screenplay: Eleanor Bergstein
Director: Emile Ardolino
Cinematography: Jeff Jur
Editor: Peter C. Frank
Music director: John Morris

Art directors: Mark Haack, Stephen J. Lineweaver
Choreography: Kenny Ortega
Makeup: David Forrest, Gilbert La Chapelle

Story: Headstrong seventeen-year-old Baby Houseman hardly expects her family's usual summer vacation in the Catskills to be momentous. But then Baby sees Johnny Castle, the resort's dance instructor, and things turn around. Johnny is facing a crisis as his dance partner and friend, Penny, is pregnant and has reluctantly decided to get an abortion. This leaves Johnny a solo act until Baby agrees to take Penny's place. She has to learn how to dance first, however, and as Johnny teaches her the choreography's sexy, seductive moves, the two fall in love. But Baby's father believes that Johnny is the one who got Penny pregnant, and he furiously orders Baby to end the relationship. Baby knows that Johnny is innocent—and with her feisty idealism and his dance talent, the two prove to Baby's father that their love is worth fighting for.

Sequel: *Dirty Dancing: Havana Nights* (2004)

Reviews:
Canby, Vincent. *New York Times,* August 21, 1987. http://movies2. nytimes. com/gst/movies/movie.html?v_id=13874 (accessed March 31, 2004).
Ebert, Roger. *Chicago Sun-Times.* August 21, 1987. www.suntimes.com/ ebert_reviews/1987/08/248895.html.
Kempley, Rita. *Washington Post,* August 21, 1987. www.washingtonpost.com/ wp-srv/style/longterm/movies/videos/dirtydancing (accessed March 21, 2004).
Matthews, Tom. "*Dirty Dancing,* Classic." *Box Office Magazine.* September, 1987. www.boxoffice.com/scripts/fiw.dll?getreview?&where=ID& term=3773 (accessed March 31, 2004).
Rhodes, Steve. All-Reviews.com. www.all-reviews.com/videos/dirty- dancing.htm (accessed March 31, 2004).
TV Guide Magazine Group. Cinebooks Database. www.tvguide.com/ movies/database/ShowMovie.asp?MI=14867 (accessed March 31, 2004).

Dollar Mambo

Mexico/Panama, 1993
Musical
80 minutes; stereo; color; Spanish

Programa Doble
Executive producer: Arturo Whaley
Producer: Ángel Amigo
Associate producers: Berta Navarro, Alejandro Springall (line producer)

FILM FACTS

Screenplay: Jaime Avilés, Paul Leduc
Director: Paul Leduc
Assistant director: Salvador Aguirre
Cinematography: Guillermo Navarro
Editor: Guillermo S. Maldonado
Music director: Eugenio Toussaint
Choreography: Marco Antonio Silva
Makeup: Guillermo del Toro

Cast: Dolores Pedro, Roberto Sosa, Raul Medina, Litico Rodriguez, Kandido Uranga, Tito Vasconcelos, Gabino Diego

Inspiration: Based on an original idea of Paul Leduc inspired from a *fait divers* mentioned in the newspapers on April 5, 1990

Story: The setting for the film is a Latin American cabaret featuring singers, comedians, and the like, with a working-class audience. The rhythm of the mambo helps define the characters, as typified against a Latin American backdrop, until one day the country is invaded by American soldiers and everything changes.

Reviews:
Internet Movie Database. http://imdb.com/title/tt0106742/ (accessed March 30, 2003).
Cinéma. Madias et Internet, June 5, 2003. http://www.diplomatie.fr/mediasociete/cinema.gb/cooperation/production/films/fds/film14.html (accessed March 30, 2004).

Getting to Know You
(Getting to Know All About You)

United States, 1999
Comedy/drama
96 minutes; color; English
SearchParty Films, ShadowCatcher Entertainment
Executive producers: Larry Estes, Scott M. Rosenfelt, David Skinner

Producers: Laura Gabbert, George LaVoo,
Associate producer: Roger Baerwolf
Available from amazon.com

FILM FACTS

Screenplay: Lisanne Skyler, Tristine Skyler
Director: Lisanne Skyler
Cinematography: Jim Denault
Editors: Julie Janata, Anthony Sherin
Art director: Katherine L. Spencer
Choreography: Luis Perez
Makeup: Susan Reilly LeHane (makeup artist as Susan Reilly)

Story: Heather Matarazzo and Michael Weston are sharing life stories while at a bus station. Matarazzo and her sibling were raised by semiprofessional ballroom dancers. The dancer lifestyle created a nomadic existence for the family. Weston tells three stories as different people wander in and out of the bus station.

Reviews:

Berardinelli, James. Colossus.net. http://moviereviews.colossus.net/movies/g/getting.html (accessed March 31, 2004).

Ebert, Roger. *Chicago Sun Times,* September 1, 2000. http://www.suntimes.com/ebert/ebert_reviews/2000/09/090101.html (accessed March 31, 2004).

Greene, Ray. Boxoffice Online Reviews. http://www.boxoffice.com/scripts/fiw.dll?GetReview&where=Name&terms=GETTING+TO+KNOW+YO (accessed March 31, 2004).

Guthman, Edward. "Film Clips Also Opening This Week." *San Francisco Chronicle,* August 11, 2000. http://www.sfgate.com/cgi-bin/article.cgi?f=/c/a/2000/08/11/DD94620.DTL#getting (accessed March 31, 2004).

Mad About Mambo

United States, 2000
Comedy/romance
92 min; Dolby Digital; color; English
First City Features; Phoenix Pictures; Plurabelle Films
Executive producers: Martin Bruce-Clayton, Gabriel Byrne
Producer: David P. Kelly
Associate producers: Christina Giffen, Amy Singer
Available from amazon.com

FILM FACTS

Screenplay: John Forte
Director: John Forte
Cinematography: Ashley Rowe
Editor: David Martin
Music director: Richard Hartley
Art directors: Colman Corish, Susie Cullen
Choreography: Kim Blank
Makeup: Andrea Finch,
Special effects: Simon Giles, Sally Clayton

Story: A lackluster Irish soccer player at an all-boys Catholic School in Belfast finds love off the soccer field when he adds dance to his life. Danny (William Ash) dreams of playing professional soccer but lacking stellar talent sets out to find any means of improving his skills. Idolizing South American stars such as Pele, Danny concludes that if he learns to dance like South Americans, the movements will carry into his play. His friends Mickey (Paul McLean), Gary (Russell Smith), and Spike (Joe Rea) have equally fantastic, though peculiar, ambitions but never imagined that Danny would resort to so drastic a plan. However, through Danny's lessons it is discovered that his natural calling may not be soccer after all. Added to this surprise, his dancing also introduces him to an attractive yet seemingly unattainable dancing partner, Lucy McLoughlin (Keri Russell). Lucy is determined to win the Regional Latin Dance Finals and though she has a boyfriend, Danny cannot help feeling that the mambo will help him earn more than just rhythm for his soccer game.

Review:

McDonagh, Maitland. *Shall We Dance?* TV Guide Magazine Group, 2004. http://www.tvguide.com/Movies/database/ShowMovie.asp?MI= 41803 (accessed March 31, 2004).

Marilyn Hotchkiss' Ballroom Dancing and Charm School

United States, 1990
Musical/comedy/short/romance/family/children's films
34 minutes; color; English
Carousel Films
Producer: Ehud Epstein
Available from kentlink.kent.edu/search/t?SEARCH=Marily+hotchkiss+ ballroom+dancing+and+charm+school

FILM FACTS

Screenplay: Randall Miller
Director: Randall Miller
Cinematography: Mike Ozier

Cast: William Hurt (Steve and voice); Michael Bower; Elden Henson; Joshua Henson (Elden Ratcliffe); Joshua Horowitz (Kenny Doolin); Teri Johnston; Karlyn Michelson; Kate Mulligan

Story: This movie illustrates the timeless story of girls versus boys. Set in the 1960s, the film is shown through the life of two young boys, Steve and Peter. The boys receive a punishment from their mothers by being sent to Marilyn Hotchkiss's Ballroom Dancing and Charm School. While enrolled, they are forced to be around the enemy—girls!

The Object of My Affection

United States, 1998
Comedy/drama/romance
111 minutes; Dolby Digital; Deluxe Color; English
Twentieth Century Fox
Producer: Laurence Mark
Associate producer: Petra Alexandria
Coproducer: Diana Pokorny
Available from amazon.com

FILM FACTS

Screenplay: Wendy Wasserstein
Director: Nicholas Hytner
Cinematography: Oliver Stapleton
Editor: Tariq Anwar
Music director: George Stapelton
Art director: Patricia Woodbridge
Choreography: Paul Pellicoro, Eleni Fotinos
Makeup: Naomi Donne, Carla White, Angel DeAngelis, Milton Buras

(Inspiration: Based on the novel, *The Object of My Affection* by Stephen McCauley

Story: Nina Borowski (Jennifer Aniston) warns a stranger, George Hanson (Paul Rudd), that he is about to be dumped by his boyfriend. Being sympathetic, Nina offers George the spare bedroom in her Brooklyn apartment. The roommates become extremely close. Eventually Nina falls in love with her gay roommate. Nina's boyfriend tolerates her relationship with her roommate until her announcement. She is pregnant and wants George to raise the baby with her instead of her boyfriend, who is the father. The film includes a dance scene in which Nina and George dance to "You were Meant for Me," which turns out to be a false ending.

Source:
Big Gun Project. DVD. http://www.foxmovies.com/theobjectofmyaffection/index.html (accessed February 11, 2005).

Shall We Dansu?
(Shall We Dance?)

1996, Japan
Comedy/drama
113 minutes (cut)/118 minutes (uncut); Dolby SR; color; Japanese
Executive producer: Yasuyoshi Tokuma
Associate producer: Yoichi Arishige
Available from amazon.com

FILM FACTS

Screenplay: Masayuki Suo
Director: Masayuki Suo
Cinematography: Naoki Kayano
Editor: Junichi Kikuchi
Choreography: Toshio Watari

Story: Shohei Sugiyama is a successful business man with a new home, wife, and teenage daughter. His life seems wonderful, but Shohei feels unsatisfied. As he commutes from work on the train, Shohei notices a woman staring forlornly from a window. Intrigued, Shohei signs up for ballroom dancing lessons in order to learn more about her. Shohei finds what he feels he has been missing in the love he develops for the graceful Mai.

Reviews:
Coleman, William P. Review of *Shall We Dance?* WPCMath 1.0, 1997. http://www.wpcmath.com/films/shallwedance/shallwedance2.html (accessed March 30, 2004).
Cannon, Damian. Review of *Shall We Dance?* Movie Reviews UK, 1998. http://www.film.unet.com/Movies/Reviews/Shall_Dance.html (accessed March 30, 2004).

Sista Dansen
(The Last Dance)

Demark/Sweden/Norway, 1993
Drama
113 minutes; Dolby; color; Swedish
Eurimages; Metronome Productions; Nordic Film and TV Fund; Sandrew
Film and Theater; Schibsted Film; Swedish Film Institute; TV 2 Gothenburg
Executive producers: Klas Olofsson, Steen Priwin
Producer: Katinka Faragó

FILM FACTS

Screenplay: Colin Nutley
Director: Colin Nutley
Cinematography: Jens Fischer
Editor: Pierre Schaffer
Music directors: Eddy Grant, Björn Isfält, Denis King
Art director: Mats Wolgers (set dresser)
Makeup: Jan Kindahl

Story: Tove and Claes Salefalk compete internationally as ballroom dancers
and so do their friends Liselott and Lennart Waltner. Their friendship is
suffering when Claes's mother's funeral occurs—the friends have not spo-
ken for some time. While at the funeral they attempt to renew their
friendship and vacation together in Barbados but unfortunately the close
proximity only makes matters worse. Everything comes to a head in
Blackpool, where a competition is being held.

Strictly Ballroom

Australia, 1992
Comedy
94 minutes; Dolby; color; English
Australian Film Finance Corporation; M & A Film Corporation
Executive producer: Antoinette Albert
Producer: Tristram Miall
Available from amazon.com

FILM FACTS

Screenplay: Baz Luhrmann, Andrew Bovell, Craig Pearce
Director: Baz Luhrmann
Cinematography: Steve Mason
Editor: Jill Bilcock

Music directors: David Hirschfelder, Johann Strauß
Art director: Martin Brown
Choreography: John 'Cha Cha' O'Connell
Makeup: Lesley Vanderwalt, Rebecca Simons, Paul Williams (hair designer)

Story: Champion ballroom dancer Scott Hastings, who believes in creating "his own steps," pairs up with beginning dancer Fran, an ugly duckling, after his regular partner leaves him. Together these two try to win the Australian Pan Pacific Championships and show the Ballroom Confederation that there are new steps to be danced.

Reviews:
Brussat, Frederick and Mary Ann Brussat. *Spirituality and Health.* http://www.rottentomatoes.com/click/movie-1045568/reviews.php? critic=columns&sortby=default&page=1&rid=290312 (accessed March 30, 2004).
Cannon, Damian. Movie Reviews UK, 1997. http://www.film.u-net.com/Movies/Reviews/Strictly_Ballroom.html (accessed March 30, 2004).
Hicks, Chris. Desertnews.com, April 9, 1993. http://www.rottentomatoes.com/click/movie-1045568/reviews.php?critic=columns&sortby=default&page=1&rid=31367 (accessed March 30, 2004).
Jardine, Dan. Apollo Guide. http://www.rottentomatoes.com/click/movie-1045568/reviews.php?critic=columns&sortby=default&page=1&rid=783836 (accessed March 30, 2004).
Maslin, Janet. "Love in a Dance Palace: Cinderella Wins Prince." *New York Times,* September 26, 1992. http://movies2.nytimes.com/gst/movies/review.html?title1=&title2=STRICTLY%20BALLROOM%20%28MOVIE%29&reviewer=Janet%20Maslin&v_id=47373 (accessed March 30, 2004).
Null, Christopher. Filmcritic.com, 2000. http://www.rottentomatoes.com/click/movie-1045568/reviews.php?critic=columns&sortby=default&page=2&rid=294948 (accessed March 30, 2003).
Puccio, John J. DVDtown.com, 18 April, 2002. http://www.rottentomatoes.com/click/movie-1045568/reviews.php?critic=columns&sortby=default&page=2&rid=307592 (accessed March 30, 2004).

Swing Kids

United States, 1993
Musical/drama
112 minutes; Dolby; Technicolor; English

Barrandov Studios/Buena Vista Home Entertainment; Buena Vista Distri-
bution Company
Executive producer: Christopher Meledandri
Producers: Mark Gordon, John Bard Manulis
Associate producer: Harry Benn
Available from amazon.com

FILM FACTS

Screenplay: Jonathan Marc Feldman
Director: Thomas Carter
Cinematography: Jerzy Zielinski
Editor: Michael R. Miller
Music director: Chris Boardman
Art directors: Tony Reading, Steve Spence
Choreography: Ryan Francois, Otis Sallid
Makeup: Paul Engelen, Colin Jamison (hair)
Special effects: Garth Inns

Story: *Swing Kids* is set in Nazi Germany and focuses on the lives of a
group of young rebels who listen to American swing music that has been
banned in Germany. As the Nazi party gains more power and their fun
takes a turn for the worse, these kids are faced with threatening choices
about right and wrong.

Tango

Denmark, 1996
Comedy
58 minutes; color; Danish
Dansk Novellefilm (DK); Film Cooperativet Danmark (DK)
Producer: Erik Clausen

FILM FACTS

Screenplay: Erik Clausen
Director: Erik Clausen
Cinematography: Torben Skjødt Jensen
Editor: Ghita Beckendorff
Special effects: Morten Green (sound editor), Jens Tang (sound)

Cast: Erik Clausen (Ole Jensen); Eduardo Galeano; Rubén Rada; Lagrima
Rios; Lucio Rosano

Story: Ole Jensen, a middle-aged Dutch man, needs some excitement in his life. Even his therapist has told him he is too dull and recommends dancing lessons, specifically tango. However, Ole Jensen has two left feet and just can't cut it on the dance floor. In a spontaneous lapse of judgement, Jensen purloins his dance instructor's plane ticket to Tango, the homeland of the famous dance, where he learns much about life.

Tango Bar

Argentina/Puerto Rico, 1988
Drama/musical
90 minutes; color; Spanish
Beco Films; Zaga Films
Executive producer: Juan Carlos Cardazzi
Producers: Juan Carlos Cardazzi, Roberto Gandara, Marcos Zurinaga

FILM FACTS

Screenplay: Juan Carlos Codazzi, Jose Pablo Feinmann, Marcos Zurinaga
Director: Marcos Zurinaga
Cinematography: Marcos Zurinaga
Editor: Pablo Mari
Art director: Maria Julia Bertotto
Choreography: Santiago Ayala, Liliana Belfiore, Doris Petroni, Carlos Rivarola, Nelida Rodriguez, Norma Viola, Nelson Avila

Cast: Raul Julia (Pedro); Valeria Lynch (Elena); Ruben Juarez (Antonio)

Story: Antonio joins his friend, who runs a bar, after being exiled from his country. They become partners in a caberet show that tells the story of the history of the tango. They soon find that they both love the same woman, and the tension between them is personified in their dances.

Review:
Kempley, Rita. *Washington Post Online.* May 6, 1989. http://www.washington post.com/wpsrv/style/longterm/movies/videos/tangobarnrkempley_ a0c9cd.htm (accessed April 3, 2004).

The Tango Lesson

U.K/Argentina/France/Japan/Germany, 1997
Romance/drama
102 minutes; Dolby; B/W, color; English, French, Spanish

Adventure Films; Arts Council of England (GB); Cinema Projects; Eurimages; European Co-Production Fund (GB); Imagica; NFC (NL); NFG Baden-Württemberg (GER); OKCK Films; PIE; Pandora Filmproduktion GmbH (GER); Sales Company; Sigma Dilm Productions (NL)
Executive producer: Sally Potter
Producer: Christopher Sheppard
Associate producers: Cat Villiers, Diane Gelon

FILM FACTS

Screenplay: Sally Potter
Director: Sally Potter
Cinematography: Robby Müller
Editor: Hervé Schneid
Music director: Sally Potter (composer)
Art director: Graciela Oderigo
Choreography: Pablo Veron
Makeup: Thi-Loan Nguyen, Chantal Leothier
Special effects: Tom Cundom, Christian Talenton

Story: The film is a fictitious adaptation of the life of maverick filmmaker Sally Potter. In the film the main character, whose name is coincidentally Sally, takes a break from her hectic screenwriting schedule to go to Paris. While in Paris, she meets a dancer named Pablo Veron who invigorates her mind, body, heart, and soul by introducing her to tango. The film chronicles the intensity of their passion for one another, which could irrevocably threaten the success of the dancing duo.

Reviews:

Ebert, Roger. *Chicago Sun-Times*, December 19, 1997. http://www.suntimes. com/ebert/ebert_reviews/1997/12/121903.html (accessed April 3, 2004).

Guthmann, Edward. "Sally Potter's Elegant *Tango*: Romantic Tale's Only Misstep is Director as Lead." *San Francisco Chronicle*, December 25, 1997. http://www.sfgate.com/cgi-bin/article.cgi?f=/c/a/1997/12/25/DD17880.DTL (accessed April 3, 2004).

McAlister, Linda Lopez. Transcript from *The Women's Show*, WMNF-FM 88.5, Tampa, FL. February 7, 1998. http://www.mith2.umd.edu/WomensStudies/FilmReviews/tango-lesson-mcalister (accessed April 3, 2004).

Notes

1. THE CONTESTED LANDSCAPE OF BALLROOM DANCE

1. Carrie Stern, "Shall We Dance?: The Participant as Performer/Spectator in Ballroom Dancing" (PhD diss., New York University, 1999); Mary Lyn Ball, "An Analysis of the Current Judging Methods Used in Competitive Ballroom, Including Comparisons to Competitive Pairs Figure Skating and Ice Dancing" (master's thesis, Brigham Young University, 1998).

2. Daniel Long's master's thesis "Qualifying for Olympic Status: The Process and Implications for Competitive Ballroom Dance" (Brigham Young University, 1999) is an invaluable source for "insider" information concerning the various organizational skirmishes involved in the road to the Olympics. Though I draw some of the context from it, I sketch a much broader cultural picture, going beyond a detailed summary of the posted minutes of various meetings, which is what Long's thesis does. Juliet McMains's dissertation "Race, Class, and Gender in the American DanceSport Industry" (University of California, 2003) comes closest to my project. Though I draw from the notion of "brownface" that she develops (that privileged groups appropriate rhetorically significant identifying characteristics from less privileged groups in order to imbue their cultural profiles with more diverse characteristics, without endangering their whiteness or their class-based privilege), our conclusions and methods differ significantly. She ultimately advocates DanceSport becoming an artistic forum and draws from her experiences as an experienced DanceSport competitor and teacher to argue for this position. I ultimately make the argument that creating multiple opportunities for funding—some arts based; others, competition and sports based—is probably the most realistic option available, and I draw not only from autoethnographic and ethnographic methods derived from my own experiences and field work, but also formal and thematic tools of film criticism.

3. Brenda Dixon Gottschild, *Waltzing in the Dark: African American Vaudeville and Race Politics in the Swing Era* (New York: St. Martin's Press, 2002).

4. Gerald Jonas, *Dancing: The Pleasure, Power and Art of Movement* (New York: Harry N. Abrams, Inc. 1992).

5. Julie Malnig. *Dancing Till Dawn: A Century of Exhibition Dance.* Reprint. (New York: New York Univeristy Press, 1995).

6. Caroline Joan Picart, *From Ballroom to DanceSport: Aesthetics, Athletics, and Body Culture* (SUNY series on Sport, Culture, and Social Relations). (Albany: State University of New York Press, 2005).

7. John Lawrence Reynolds, *Ballroom Dancing: The Romance, Rhythm and Style* (San Diego: Advanced Global Distribution, 1998).

8. Dorothy A. Truex, *The Twenty Million Dollar Give-Away: An Expose of Competitive Ballroom Dancing* (Philadelphia: Xlibris Corporation, 2001).

9. Chaim Perelman, *The Realm of Rhetoric* (Notre Dame, Ind.: University of Notre Dame Press, 1982); Chaim Perelman and Lucie Olbrechts-Tyteca, *The New Rhetoric: A Treatise on Argumentation* (Notre Dame: University of Notre Dame Press, 1969).

10. Paul Stoller, *Sensuous Scholarship* (Philadelphia: University of Pennsylvania Press, 1997), xv.

11. Prior work on the insider-outsider concept has been published in "Living the Hyphenated Edge: Autoethnography, Hybridity and Aesthetics," in *Ethnographically Speaking: Autoethnography, Literature, and Aesthetics*, eds. Arthur P. Bochner and Carolyn Ellis (Walnut Creek: AltaMira Press (Rowman and Littlefield), 2002), 258–273. See also *Inside Notes from the Outside* (Lanham, MD: Lexington Books (Rowman and Littlefield), 2004).

12. Maria Lugones "On Borderlands/La Frontera: An Interpretative Essay," *Hypatia* 7 (1992): 34.

13. Gloria Anzaldua, *Borderlands/La Frontera.* (San Francisco: Aunt Lute Books, 1987).

14. Lugones, 35.

15. For a prior example of work published in this area, refer to: Caroline Joan (Kay) S. Picart, "Dancing Through Different Worlds: Virtual Emotions and the Gendered Body in Ballroom Dance," *Qualitative Inquiry*, 8 (2002): 348-361.

16. Brenda Dixon Gottschild, "Some Thoughts on Choreographing History," in *Meaning in Motion: New Cultural Studies in Dance*, ed. Jane C. Desmond (Durham, N.C.: Duke University Press, 1997), 169.

17. Elizabeth Burns, *Theatricality: A Study of Convention in the Theatre and in Social Life* (New York, NY: Harper & Row, 1973).

18. Erving Goffman, *The Presentation of Self in Everyday Life* (New York, NY: Anchor Books, 1959).

19. Barbara Browning, *Samba: Resistance in Motion* (Bloomington, IN: Indiana University Press, 1995); Jane K. Cowan, *Dance and the Body Politic in Northern Greece* (Princeton: Princeton University Press, 1990); Diane Freedman, "Wife, Widow, Woman: Roles of an Anthropologist in a Transylvanian Village," in *Women in the Field: Anthropological Experiences*, ed. Peggy Golde (Berkeley: University of California Press, 1968), 333–358; Sally Ann Ness, *Body, Movement, and Culture: Kinesthetic and Visual Symbolism in a Philippine Community* (Philadelphia: University of Pennsylvania, 1992). In addition to her earlier work on

contact improvisation, Cohen Bull joined writers from various disciplines, all of whom incorporate this perspective in their work, in the 1997 anthology *Meaning in Motion: New Cultural Studies of Dance*. Cohen Bull's primary text on contact improvisation, *Sharing the Dance: Contact Improvisation and American Culture* (Madison: University of Wisconsin Press, 1990), appears under the name Cynthia Novack; Jane C. Desmond, ed., *Meaning in Motion: New Cultural Studies of Dance* (Durham: Duke University Press, 1997).

20. James Clifford, "On Ethnographic Authority," in *The Predicament of Culture* (Cambridge, MA: Harvard University Press, 1988); Michael Jackson, *Paths Toward a Clearing: Radical Empiricism and Ethnographic Inquiry* (Bloomington: Indiana University Press, 1989).

21. An earlier version of this section appeared in "Dance as Forms of Space, Embodiment and Culture," *Korea Times*, February 17, 1993, sec. 4A.

22. *Ballroom Dance Survey Questionnaire*, Tallahassee Arthur Murray Studio, December 2000–April 2001.

23. *Ballroom Dance Survey Questionnaire*, December 2000-April 2001.

24. Ibid.

25. *Ballroom Dance Survey Questionnaire*, November 2003.

26. *Ballroom Dance Survey Questionnaire*, 2001.

27. Ibid.

28. Ibid.

29. Ibid.

30. *Ballroom Dance Survey Questionnaire*, 2003.

31. *Ballroom Dance Survey Questionnaire*, 2001.

32. Ibid.

33. Ibid.

34. Ibid.

35. Ibid..

36. Ibid.

37. Ibid.

38. Ibid.

39. Ibid.

40. Ibid.

41. Ibid.

42. *Ballroom Dance Survey Questionnaire*, 2003.

43. *Ballroom Dance Survey Questionnaire*, 2001.

44. Ibid.

45. Ibid.

46. Ibid.

47. Ibid.

48. Ibid.

49. Ibid.

50. Ibid.

51. Julie Taylor, *Paper Tangos* (Durham and London: Duke University Press (Public Planet Books), 1998), 86-87; italics added.

52. *Ballroom Dance Survey Questionnaire*, 2001.

2. DANCING THROUGH DIFFERENT WORLDS

1. Susanne K. Langer, *"Virtual Powers" and "The Magic Circle,"* in Roger Copeland and Marshall Cohen, eds. *What Is Dance?* (New York, NY: Oxford University Press, 1983).

2. Don McDonagh, *Martha Graham* (New York: Popular Library/Praeger, 1973), 245.

3. Sally Peters, "From Eroticism to Transcendance: Ballroom Dance and the Female Body," in *The Female Body: Figures, Styles, Speculations,* ed. Laurence Goldstein (Ann Arbor: University of Michigan Press), 149.

4. McDonagh, 26.

5. Peters, 154.

6. Laban is cited by Sally Peters, "From Eroticism to Transcendence: Ballroom Dance and the Female Body," *The Female Body: Figures, Styles, Speculations* (Ann Arbor, MI: Michigan University Press, 1994).

7. Susanne Langer, "Virtual Powers," in *What is Dance?,* eds. Roger Copeland and Marshall Cohen (Oxford, England and New York: Oxford University Press, 1983), 30–31.

8. Zali Gurevitch, "The Tongue's Break Dance: Theory, Poetry, and the Critical Body," *Sociological Quarterly* 40 (1999): 525–542.

9. Sally Ann Ness, *Body, Movement and Culture; Kinesthetic and Visual Symbolism in a Philippine Community* (Philadelphia: University of Pennsylvania Press, 1992), 3.

10. Paul Stoller, *The Taste of Ethnographic Things: The Senses of Anthropology* (Philadelphia: University of Pennsylvania Press, 1989), 54-55, 142–156.

3. BALLROOM DANCE AND THE MOVIES

1. Martha P. Nochimson, *Screen Couple Chemistry: The Power of 2* (Austin: University of Texas Press), 146–147.

2. Arlene Croce, *The Fred Astaire and Ginger Rogers Book* (New York: Galahad Books, 1934), 17.

3. Tom Matthews, "Dirty Dancing," *Boxoffice Online Reviews,* September 1987, 1, http://www.boxoffice.com/scripts/fiw.dlll?GetReview?where=IDterms=3773 (accessed March 21, 2004).

4. Croce, 14.

5. Mary Russo, *The Female Grotesque: Risk, Excess and Modernity* (New York: Routledge, 1994).

6. Steve Rhodes, review of *Dirty Dancing,* Rec.arts.movies.reviews (newsgroup) de.rec.film.kritiken (for German reviews), 1987, 1, http://www.imdb.com/Reviews/97/9736 (accessed March 21, 2004).

7. Pete Croatto, review of *Dirty Dancing,* 2003, 2, http://www.filmcritic.com/misc/emporium.nsf/0/C6bb593b6e38379e88256dfe0017?openDocument (accessed March 21, 2004).

8. Rhodes, 2.

9. Laura Clifford, review of *Dirty Dancing: Havana Nights,* Rec.arts. movies.reviews (newsgroup) de.rec.film.kritiken (for German reviews), 2004, 1, http://www.imdb.com/Reviews/371/37151 (accessed March 16, 2004).

10. Eleaner Ringel Gillespie, "I Didn't Have the Time of My Life and I Don't Think You Will, Either," Cox News Service, 1, http://www.accessAtlanta.com (accessed March 16, 2004).

11. Ibid.

12. Tim Knight, review of *Dirty Dancing: Havana Nights,* Reel.com, 1, http://reel.com/movie.asp?MID=137723&Tab=reviews&CID=13 (accessed March 16, 2004).

13. Carla Meyer, "Learning from Señor Swayze: *Dirty Dancing* Transported from Catskills to Cuba," *San Francisco Chronicle,* February 27, 2004, 1, http://sfgate.com/cgi-bin/article.cgi?f=/c/a/2004/02/27/DDG9058G6N1.DTL&type=movies (accessed March 16, 2004).

14. Sean Axmaker, "Hot music drives *Dirty Dancing: Havana Nights* Beyond the Ordinary," *Seattle Post-Intelligencer,* February 27, 2004, 1, http://seattlepi.nwsource.com/movies/162249_dirty27q.html (accessed March 16, 2004).

15. Harvey S. Karten, review of *Dirty Dancing: Havana Nights,* Rec.arts. movies.reviews (newsgroup), de.rec.film.kritiken (for German reviews), 2004, 1, http://www.imdb.com/Reviews/371/37158 (accessed March 16, 2004).

16. Max Hoffman, review of *Strictly Ballroom, Internet Movie Data Base,* 1992, 1, http://www.imdb.com/Reviews/17/1744 (accessed March 24, 2004).

17. Rita Kempley, review of *Strictly Ballroom, Washington Post,* February 26, 1993, 1, http://www.washingtonpost.com/wp-srv/style/longterm/movies/videos/strictlyballroompgkempley_aØa35f.htm (accessed February 26, 1993).

18. Evan Hunt, review of *Strictly Ballroom, The Web,* 1992, 1, http://www.imdb.com/Reviews/18/1862 (accessed March 24, 2004).

19. Roger Ebert, "Strictly Ballroom," *Chicago Sun-Times,* February 26, 1993, 1, http://www.rogerebert.suntimes.com/apps/pbcs.dlll/article?AID=19930226/Reviews/302260302/1023 (accessed March 16, 2004).

20. Desson Howe, review of *Strictly Ballroom, Washington Post,* February 26, 1993, 1, http://www.washingtonpost.com/wp-srv/style/longterm/movies/videos/strictlyballroompghowe_aØaf70.htm (accessed March 16, 2004).

21. Mark R. Leeper, review of *Strictly Ballroom,* Rec.arts.movies.reviews (newsgroup), de.rec.film.kritiken (for German reviews), 1992, 1, http://www.imdb.com/Reviews/18/1861 (accessed March 16, 2004).

22. Hoffmann, 1.

23. Mueller, John E. *Astaire Dancing: The Musical Films.* (New York: Knopf, 1985).

24. Ebert, 1.

25. James Berardinelli, review of *Tango,* 1, http://movie-reviews.colossus.net/movies/t/tango98.html (accessed March 21, 2004).

26. Mueller, 58.

27. Mueller, 71.

28. Stanley Cavell, *Pursuits of Happiness: The Hollywood Comedy of Remarriage* (Cambridge, MA: Harvard University Press, 1984).

29. James Berardinelli, review of *The Tango Lesson,* 1–2, http://movie-reviews.colossus.net/movies/t/tango.html (accessed March 21, 2004).

30. Jonathan Williams, review of *The Tango Lesson,* Rec.arts.movies.reviews (newsgroup), de.rec.film.kritiken (for German reviews), 1998, 2, http://www.imdb.com/Reviews/110/11075 (accessed March 21, 2004).

31. Roger Ebert, review of *Tango, Chicago Sun-Times,* December 19, 1997, 1998, 2, http://rogerebert.suntimes.com/apps/pbcs.dlll/article?AID=/19990326/Reviews/903260306/1023 (accessed March 21, 2004).

32. Paul Tatara, "*Shall We Dance* a Graceful Tale of Middle Age Yearnings," *Showbiz,* July 19, 1997, 1, http://edition.cnn.com/showbiz/9707/19/review.shall.dance/ (accessed March 21, 2004).

33. Steve Rhodes, review of Shall We Dansu? Rec.arts.movies.reviews (newsgroup), de.rec.film.kritiken (for German reviews), 1997, http://www.imdb.com/Reviews/84/8463 (accessed March 21, 2004).

34. Jasper Sharp, review of *Shall We Dance? Midnight Eye: The Latest and Best in Japanese Cinema,* March 20, 2001, 1, http://midnighteye.com/features/bestof2002.shtml (accessed March 20, 2001).

35. Roger Ebert, review of *Shall We Dance?, Chicago Sun-Times,* October 15, 2004, 1, http://rogerebert.suntimes.com/apps/pbcs.dlll/article?AID=/200041014/REVIEWS/40921008/1023 (accessed March 21, 2004).

36. Stephen Hunter, review of *Shall We Dance?, Washington Post Critic's Corner,* October 15, 2004. 1, http://www.washingtonpost.com/wp-dyn/articles/A34310-2004Oct15.html (accessed March 21, 2004).

37. Donna Bowman, review of *Dance with Me, Nashville Scene,* September 14, 1998, 1, http://www.filmvault.com/filmvault/nash/d/dancewithme1.html (accessed September 14, 1998).

38. Kay Dickinson, review of *Dance With Me, Sight and Sound,* British Film Institute, May 1999, 1, http://www.bfi.org.uk/sightandsound/reviews/details.php?id=99 (accessed April 28, 2004).

39. Barbara Schulgasser, "Accept This Invitation to the Dance," *San Francisco Examiner,* August 21, 1998, 1, Originally printed by the *Hearst Examiner,* http://www.sfgate.com/cgi-bin/article.cgi?f=/e/a/1998/08/21/WEEKEND.5528.dtl (accessed March 21, 2004).

40. Mueller, 6.

41. Croce, 26–27.

42. Susanne Topper, *Astaire and Rogers* (New York: Nordon Publications, 1976), 50.

43. Nochimson, 140.

44. Mueller, 57.

45. Fred Astaire and Bob Thomas, *Astaire, the Man, the Dancer: The Life of Fred Astaire* (New York: St. Martin's, 1984), 112.

4. PAVING THE ROAD TO THE OLYMPICS

1. "DanceSport and the Olympics: IOC Grants Full Recognition to DanceSport." *DanceScape. TV,* http://www.dancescape.com/info/world/index.html (accessed June 1, 2002).

2. David Savoy and Sharon Savoy, "An Uplifting Experience at the Olympics," *Dance Magazine* 75, no. 1 (January 2001): 72.

3. Don Herbison-Evans, "Dancing in the Olympics 2000 Closing Ceremony," http://linus.it.uts.edu.au/~don/pubs/olympics.html (accessed June 1, 2002).

4. "Dancing to the Olympics," *Businessworld*, June 11, 1999.

5. A list of the acronyms of relevant dance organizations and their full names, brief descriptions and contact information, when this is available, is included at the end of the book.

6. Long, 32.

7. Ibid., 40.

8. Ibid., 42.

9. Ibid., 38–39.

10. Ibid., 40.

11. Ibid., 44.

12. Ibid., 47–51.

13. Ibid., 53.

14. Pover 28e/1991:1 cited in Long, 79.

15. Long, 103–104.

16. Rudolf Bauman, "The IDSF President's Vision for the Near Future," *Dance News* (June 1999), http://www.pingui.com/mainotIDSF2I.htm (accessed June 1, 2002).

17. Long, 126.

18. Johannes Biba, "Games of the XXVII Olympiad, Sydney, 2000; DanceSport Couples Have Been Invited to Contribute to the Closing Ceremony," May 23, 2000, IDSF press release, October 2000, http://www.idsf.net/press00/idsf0010.htm (accessed February 28, 2004).

19. Delerine Munzeer, *Sunday Observer*, February 18, 2001. "Footworks Presents DanceSport 2001 Championships." http://www.lanka.net/lakehouse/2001/02/18/mag05.html (accessed March 2005).

20. Christopher L. Brinkley, "DanceSport in the Olympics: The State of Affairs before 2000," 1–2, http://www.eijkhout.net/rad/dance_other/olympic.html (accessed April 23, 2004).

21. Johannes Biba, "IOC: DanceSport Is On-Track," IDSF press release 14/02, http://www.usabda.org/press_center/olympic_updates/index.cfm (accessed March 4, 2004).

22. Ibid.

23. Johannes Biba, "IOC: Green Light for DanceSport," IDSF press release 13/02, http://www.idsf.net/press02/idsf0213.htm (accessed February 9, 2002).

24. Rudolf Baumann, "In New Year's Message, IDSF President Baumann Blames WD&DSC Management," January 1, 2003, http://www.dancingusa.com/pages/873231/ (accessed March 2, 2004).

25. Robin Chee, "13th Asian Games, Bangkok," December 1998, in *Dance RpMerleon*, http://www.rpmerleon.com/articles/9812asian_games.php (accessed February 27, 2004).

26. Christopher L. Brinkley, "What Happened in 2000?" http://www.eijkhout.net/rad/dance_other/olympic.html (accessed January 20, 2004).

27. Rudolf Baumann, "New Year's Message," 1.

28. Rudi Hubert, "DanceSport to the Olympics in 1999," January 15, 1998, 8, http://www.idsf.net/press99/games.htm (accessed March 2, 2004).

29. David Watts, "Love of Sport Takes a High Dive," 1998, cited in "RSG: Art and Sport?," http://www.contortionhomepage.com/rsg_essay.html (accessed April 26, 2004).

30. Jonathan Bell, "Ballroom Dancing Is Not a Sport (So Why Is It in the Gay Games?)," *Outsports.com*, August 27, 2001, http://www.outsports.com/columns/bell/whatissport20010827.htm (accessed August 27, 2001).

31. "Ballroom Blitz Splits Olympic Powerbrokers," *Sidney Morning Herald*, http://www.smh.com.au/news/0012/13/text/sport13.html (accessed June 1, 2002).

32. Brinkley, "DanceSport in the Olympics," 2.

33. Ibid.

34. Ibid.

35. Christopher Hawkins and Hazel Newberry, "Chris and Hazel's Olympic Dream," http://www.danceuniverse.co.kr/news/hawkins.htm (accessed April 26, 2004).

36. Jill Fraser, "Let's Dance. It's Great Sport," *Herald Sun*, Melbourne, Australia, December 7, 2001, 94.

37. "Is DanceSport a 'Sport'?," Canadian Amateur DanceSport Association, http://www.dancesport.ca/content-php?SectionID=1&ContentID=5 (accessed June 1, 2004).

38. Ibid.

39. Nell Raven, "Taking a Few Steps to Fitness," *Edinburgh Evening News*, October 24, 2003, http://forum.criticaldance.com/cgi-bin/ultimatebb.cgi?ubb=get_topic?f=!l&t=øø2ø44 (accessed January 7, 2004).

40. "Look Out Olympics . . . Here Comes Dancesport," http://web.uvic.ca/akeller/e240/Mag/mageg/dancing.html (accessed June 1, 2002).

41. Ibid.

42. Ibid.

43. William Porter, "Competitive Dancers Having a Ball," *Denver Post*, January 27, 2002, http://denverPost.com (accessed April 26, 2004).

44. Stuart Nichols, "Is Ballroom Dancing A Sport? This One Man Says So," Outsports.com, http://www.outsports.com/letters/dancesport20011012.htm (accessed January 23, 2004).

45. E. M. Swift, "Calling Arthur Murray: Ballroom Dancing Has as Much Right to Be in the Olympics as, Say Rhythm Gymnastics," *Sports Illustrated*, April 24, 1995, 72.

46. Raven, 1.

47. Ibid., 1–2.

48. John Lawrence Reynolds, *Ballroom Dancing: The Romance, Rhythm and Style* (San Diego, CA: Laurel Glen Publishing, 1998), 139.

49. Ibid.

50. Ibid.

51. Ibid.

52. John A. Lucas, *Future of the Olympic Games* (Champagne, IL: Human Kinetics Books, 1992).

53. Ellington Darden, *Olympic Athletes Ask Questions about Exercise and Nutrition* (New York: Aperture Books, 1977).

54. Brian Parkes, "Ballroom Dancing, a Gentle Sport?," http://www.dance sport.|v/eng/fun/articles/isdance.htm (accessed June 1, 2002).

55. Reynolds, 128.

56. John Derbyshire, review of *Shall We Dance?*," *National Review*, October 26, 1998, 58–59, http://www.findarticles.com/cf_0/m1282/1998_Oct_26/53093912/p1/article.jhtml (accessed October 26, 1998).

57. Castillo Rangel, "Athleticism in Dancing," http://www.webspawner.com/users/udsc/atheletism.html (accessed April 26, 2004).

58. Chloe Diski, "Mark Ballas and Julianne Hough—Dancers," *The Observer*, March 3, 2002, http://www.observer.co.uk/osm/story/0,6903,658940,00.html (accessed April 27, 2004).

59. Swift, 72.

60. Ibid.

61. *Webster's Ninth New Collegiate Dictionary*, s.v. "sport." Older edition.

62. *Webster's Third New International Dictionary*, s.v. "sport." 3rd edition.

63. "Samba, Rumba and Gold," *Maclean's*, April 27, 1998, 2.

64. Joanna Nathan, "Dance, Billiards, or Boules. What Next for the Olympics?" CNN.com, September 24, 2000, http://www.cnn.com/2000/WORLD/europe/09/21/olympics.newsports (accessed March 2005).

65. "Ballroom Blitz Splits Olympic Powerbrokers."

66. Hawkins and Newberry.

67. Brinkley, 3.

68. Fraser, 94.

69. "Samba, Rumba and Gold."

70. Mike Connolly, "Viewpoint: Sport or Not a Sport?" *Observer Online*, February 18, 2002, 2, http://www.nd.edu/~observer/02182002/Inside/O.htmlj (accessed January 7, 2004).

71. *A & E World Standard Championships*, 2001 and *A & E World Latin DanceSport Championships*, 2001.

72. United States Amateur Ballroom Dancers Association, Northern California Chapter, *Spectator's Guide to Amateur Dance Competition*, http://www.usabda-norcal.org/guide.html (accessed February 26, 2004).

73. "Make a Date with Dance," *Dispatch Online*, September 15, 2000, http://www.dispatch.co.za/2000/09/15/features/DANCE.HTM (accessed April 26, 2004).

74. K. C. Patrick, "Orphans and Olympians," *Dance Magazine*, February 2002, http://www.findarticles.com/cf_0/m1083/2_76/82322492/print.jhtml, 1 (accessed February 25, 2004).

75. Fraser, 94.

76. "DanceSport and the Olympics: IOC Grants Full Recognition to DanceSport," *DanceScape.TV*, http://www.dancescape.com/info/world/index.html (accessed June 1, 2004).

77. "About IMG and TWI," *DanceScapeTV*, http://www.dancescape.com/info/world/index.html (accessed April 26, 2004).

78. "Cheater, Cheater: The Worst Cases of Sports Cheating; Tonya Harding." CBC Sports Online (accessed March 2005).

79. "A New Future for the DanceSport with IMG," http://www.danceplaza.com/dancesport.shtml (accessed April 26, 2004).

80. Reynolds, 139.

81. Ibid., 154.

82. "A New Future for the DanceSport with IMG."

83. "GTV DanceSport," *GoodLife TV Network*, http://www.goodtv.com/programming/dance.html (accessed March 4, 2002).

84. Yap Koon Hong, "Guys, Here's a Modest, Important Step Towards a Sporting Centre," *The Strait Times*, March 4, 2002, http://straitstimes.asia1.com.sg/columnist/0,1886,300-78539,00.html (accessed June 1, 2002).

85. Werner Braun, "World-Wide TV-Distribution of IDSF/IMG Event," IDSF press release 22/98, May 30, 1998, http://www.idsf.net/press98/idsf9822.htm (accessed April 26, 2004).

86. Braun.

87. Franz Lidz, "Dancing in the Garden," *Sports Illustrated*, September 27, 1999, 76.

88. "DanceSport Scores Big on ESPN," *DanceMagazine*, March 2000, http://www.findarticles.com/p/articles/mi_m1083/is_3_74/ai_59870972 (accessed April 26, 2004).

89. Suzanne Carbone, "Melbourne: It's the Place to Take Your Partner," September 15, 2003, *The Age*, http://www.theage.com.au/articles/2003/09/14/1063478065270.html?oneclick=true (accessed January 7, 2004).

90. Swift, 72.

5. PACKAGING FANTASY AND MORALITY

1. Sean O'Connor, "Feel the Rhythm of the Music," *The Teacher*, June 2001, http://www.teacher.co.za/200106/01-sport.html (accessed April 28, 2004).

2. Colm Wynne, DanceSportIreland.org, April 1993, http://www.dancesportireland.org/features.htm (accessed June 1, 2002).

3. John Lawrence Reynolds, *Ballroom Dancing: The Romance, Rhythm and Style* (San Diego, CA: Laurel Glen Publishing, 1998), 18.

4. Alexandra Polier, "New Form of Ballroom Dancing Leaves Ginger Rogers in the Dust," Columbia News Service, May 8, 2002, 1, http://www.jrn.columbia.edu/studentwork/cns/2002-05-08/604.asp (accessed May 8, 2002).

5. Juliet E. McMains, "Brownface: Representations of Latin-ness in DanceSport," *Dance Research Journal*, 33, no. 2 (winter 2001/2002): 57, 59.

6. Ibid., 54–71.

7. Richard Dyer, *White* (New York: Routledge, 1997).

8. Dyer, 49.

9. Abigail M. Feder-Kane, "A Radiant Smile from the Lovely Lady: Overdetermined Femininity in 'Ladies' Figure Skating," in *Reading Sport: Critical Essays on Power and Representation*, ed. Susan Birrell and Mary G. McDonald (Boston: Northeastern University Press, 2000), 206–233.

10. Feder-Kane, 209.

11. Television broadcast, *A & E World Standard DanceSport Championships*, October 28, 2001.

12. Ibid.

13. Feder-Kane, 215.

14. *A & E World Standard DanceSport Championships*, 2001.

15. McMains, "Race, Class, and Gender in the American DanceSport Industry," 208.

16. Marta Savigliano, PhD diss., Riverside: University of California, August 2003, *Tango: The Political Economy of Passion* (Boulder, CO: Westview Press, 1994), 40–53.

17. McMains, "Race, Class, and Gender," 210.

18. Ibid., 211.

19. *A & E World Latin DanceSport Championship*, 2001.

20. Ibid.

21. "Interview with Hawkins & Newberry," http://www.dancersplanet.com/ (accessed February 27, 2004).

22. *A & E World Standard DanceSport Championships*, 2001.

23. Ibid.

24. Joseph Berger, "The Russians Are Coming, Stepping Lightly," *New York Times*, June 11, 2003, 13, *Johnson's Russia List* 7219, 1–3, http://www.cdi.org/russia/johnson/7219-13.cfm (accessed April 28, 2004).

25. Ibid., 1.

26. Ibid., 2.

27. Ibid.

28. Ibid., 3.

29. McMains, "Brownface," 62.

30. Ibid.

31. "The Sole Saver," http://www.thesolesaver.com/ (accessed March 4, 2004).

6. *QUO VADIS?*

1. Arthur Koestler, *Janus: A Summing Up* (London: Hutchinson, 1978), 112–113. Other works that elaborate on similar themes are Arthur Koestler, *Insight and Outlook: An Inquiry into the Common Foundations of Science, Art and Social Ethics* (New York: MacMillan, 1949), and Koestler, *The Ghost in the Machine* (New York: MacMillan, 1967).

2. Koestler, *Janus*, 129.

3. Juliet McMains, "Race, Class, and Gender in the American DanceSport Industry," (PhD diss., University of California, 2003), 265.

4. Desson Howe, review of *Strictly Ballroom, Washington Post*, February 26, 1993, 2, http://washingtonpost.com/wp-sr/style/longterm/movies/videos/strictlyballroompghowe_aøaf7ø.htm (accessed March 16, 2004).

5. Roger Ebert, review of *Strictly Ballroom, Chicago Sun-Times*, February 26, 1993, 1, http://www.rogerebert.suntimes.com/apps/pbcs.dlll/article?AID=/19930226/REVIEWS/302260302/1023 (accessed March 16, 2004).

6. Geoffrey Macnab, review of *Tango, Sight and Sound*, August 1999, British Film Institute, 2, http://www.bfi.org.uk/sightandsound/reviews/details.php?id=179 (accessed March 21, 2004).

7. See Susanne Topper, *Astaire and Rogers* (New York: Leisure Books, 1976), 83–85.

8. *Burn the Floor*, DVD/Authority, 2000, , http://www.dvdauthority.com/reviews.asp?ReviewID=495 (accessed March 31, 2004).

9. Frederic Brussat and Mary Ann Brussat, review of *Burn the Floor, Spirituality and Health*, http://www.rottentomatoes.com/click/movie-1094642/reviews.php?critic=all&sortby=default&page=1&rid=294174 (accessed March 31, 2004).

10. Norman Short, review of *Burn the Floor*, DVD Review, 2000, http://www.dvdverdict.com/reviews/burnfloor.php (accessed March 31, 2004).

11. Ibid., 1.

Bibliography

A & E World Latin DanceSport Championships. (2001). Ljubliana, Slovenia. Hosted by Clive Phillips and Suzanne Somers.

A & E World Standard Championships. (2001). Miami, FL. Hosted by Clive Phillips and Suzanne Somers.

"A New Future for the DanceSport with IMG." http://www.danceplaza.com/dancesport.shtml (accessed April 26, 2004).

"About IMG and TWI." DanceScapeTV. http://www.dancescape.com/info/world/index.html (accessed April 26, 2004).

Anzaldua, Gloria. *Borderlands/La Frontera.* San Francisco: Aunt Lute Books, 1987.

Astaire, Fred, and Bob Thomas. *Astaire, the Man, the Dancer: The Life of Fred Astaire.* New York: St. Martin's, 1984.

Axmaker, Sean. "Hot Music Drives 'Dirty Dancing: Havana Nights' Beyond the Ordinary." *Seattle Post-Intelligencer,* February 27, 2004. http://seattlepi.nwsource.com/movies/162249_dirty27q.html (accessed March 16, 2004).

Ball, Mary Lyn. "An Analysis of the Current Judging Methods Used in Competitive Ballroom, Including Comparisons to Competitive Pairs Figure Skating and Ice Dancing." Master's thesis, Brigham Young University, 1998.

"Ballroom Blitz Splits Olympic Powerbrokers." http://www.smh.com.au/news/0012/13/text/sport13.html (accessed June 1, 2002).

Ballroom Dance Survey Questionnaire. Tallahassee Arthur Murray Studio, December 2000–April 2001.

Ballroom Dance Survey Questionnaire. Tallahassee Arthur Murray Studio, November 2003.

Baumann, Rudolf. "The IDSF President's Vision for the Near Future." *Dance News,* June 1999. http://www.pingui.com/mainotIDSF2I.htm (accessed June 1, 2002).

———. "In New Year's Message, IDSF President Baumann Blames WD&DSC Management." January 1, 2003. http://www.dancingusa.com/pages/873231/ (accessed March 4, 2004).

Bell, Jonathan. "Ballroom Dancing Is Not a Sport (So Why Is It in the Gay Games?)." *Outsports.com*. http://www.outsports.com/columns/bell/whatis sport20010827. htm (accessed April 26, 2004).

Berardinelli, James. Review of *Tango*. 1998. http://movie-reviews.colossus.net/ movies/t/tango98.html (accessed March 21, 2004).

———. Review of *The Tango Lesson*. http://movie-reviews.colossus.net/movies/t/ tango.html (accessed March 21, 2004).

Berger, Joseph. "The Russians Are Coming, Stepping Lightly." *New York Times*, June 11, 2003. No. 13, *Johnson's Russia List* 7219. http://www.cdi.org/russia/ johnson/7219-13.cfm.

Biba, Johannes. "Games of the XXVII Olympiad, Sydney, 2000; DanceSport Couples Have Been Invited to Contribute to the Closing Ceremony." IDSF press release 10/2000, May 23, 2000. http://www.idsf.net/press00/idsf0010.htm (accessed February 28, 2004).

———. "IOC: DanceSport Is On-Track." IDSF press release 14/02. http:// www.usabda.org/press_center/olympic_updates/index.cfm (accessed March 4, 2004).

———. "IOC: Green Light for DanceSport." IDSF press release 13/02, February 9, 2002. http://www.idsf.net/press02/idsf0213.htm (accessed March 2, 2004).

Blumenfeld-Jones, Donald. "Dance as a Mode of Research Representation." *Qualitative Inquiry* 1 (1995): 3291–3401.

Bowman, Donna. "Dance with Me." *Nashville Scene*, September 14, 1998. http:// www.filmvault.com/filmvault/nash/d/dancewithme1.html.

Braun, Werner. "World-Wide TV-Distribution of IDSF/IMG Event." IDSF press release 22/98, May 30, 1998. http://www.idsf.net/press98/idsf9822.htm (accessed April 26, 2004).

Brinkley, Christopher L. "DanceSport in the Olympics: The State of Affairs before 2000." http://www.eijkhout.net/rad/dance_other/olympic.html (accessed April 26, 2004).

———. "What Happened in 2000?" http://www.eijkhout.net/rad/dance_other/ olympic.html (accessed January 20, 2004).

Browning, Barbara. *Samba: Resistance in Motion*. Bloomington, IN: Indiana University Press, 1995.

Brussat, Frederic, and Mary Ann Brussat. Review of *Burn the Floor*. *Spirituality and Health*. http://www.spiritualhealth.com/newsh/items/moviereview/item_ 2200.htm (accessed March 31, 2004).

Bull, Cohen. *Sharing the Dance: Contact Improvisation and American Culture*. Madison: University of Wisconsin Press, 1990.

Burns, Elizabeth. *Theatricality: A Study of Convention in the Theatre and in Social Life*. New York: Harper & Row, 1973.

Burn the Floor. Directed by David Mallet. Universal; MCA, 2000.

Carbone, Suzanne. "Melbourne: It's the Place to Take Your Partner." *The Age*. http:// www.theage.com.au/articles/2003/09/14/1063478065270.html?one click=true (accessed January 7, 2004).

Cavell, Stanley. *Pursuits of Happiness: The Hollywood Comedy of Remarriage*. Cambridge, MA: Harvard University Press, 1984.

Chee, Robin. "13ᵗʰ Asian Games, Bangkok." In *Dance RpMerleon*, December 1998. http://www.rpmerleon.com/articles/9812asian_games.php (accessed February 27, 2004).

"Chris and Hazel's Olympic Dream." *The Dance Teacher*, May 1998, 161–163. http://www.dancers.demon.co.uk/olymp.htm (accessed April 26, 2004).

Clifford, Laura. Review of *Dirty Dancing: Havana Nights*. Rec.arts.movies.reviews (newsgroup); de.rec.film.kritiken (for German reviews), 2004. http://www.imdb.com/Reviews/371/37151 (accessed March 16, 2004).

———. "On Ethnographic Authority." In *The Predicament of Culture*. Cambridge, MA: Harvard University Press, 1988.

Connolly, Mike. "Viewpoint: Sport or Not a sport?" *Observer Online*, February 18, 2002. http://www.nd.edu/~observer/02182002/Inside/ø.html (accessed January 7, 2004).

Cook, John. "Outside Money Finding Way to Seattle." *Seattle Post Intelligencer*, September 29, 2000. http://seattlepi.nwsource.com/business/vc291.shtml (accessed April 26, 2004).

Cowan, Jane K. *Dance and the Body Politic in Northern Greece*. Princeton, NJ: Princeton University Press, 1990.

Croatto, Pete. Review of *Dirty Dancing*. http://www.filmcritic.com/misc/emporium.nsf/0/c6bb593b6e38379e88256dfeou7ace1?OpenDocument (accessed March 21, 2004).

Croce, Arlene. *The Fred Astaire and Ginger Rogers Book*. New York: Galahad Books, 1934.

"DanceSport and the Olympics: IOC Grants Full Recognition to DanceSport." DanceScape.TV. http://www.dancescape.com/info/world/index.html (accessed June 1, 2004).

"DanceSport an Olympic Sport." http://www.eijkhout.net/rad/dance_other/olympic.html (accessed June 1, 2002).

"DanceSport Scores Big on ESPN." *DanceMagazine*, March 2000. http://www.findarticles.com/cf_dls/m1083/3_74/59870972/print.jhtml (accessed April 26, 2004).

"Dancing to the Olympics." *Businessworld*, June 11, 1999.

Darden, Ellington. *Olympic Athletes Ask Questions about Exercise and Nutrition*. New York: Aperture Books, 1977.

Derbyshire, John. Review of *Shall We Dance? National Review*, October 26, 1998, 58–59. http://olimu.com/Journalism/Texts/Commentary/Ballroom.htm (accessed October 26, 1998).

Dickinson, Kay. Review of *Dance With Me. Sight and Sound*, May 1999. http://www.bfi.org.uk/sightandsound/reviews/details.php?id=99 (accessed April 28, 2004).

Dirty Dancing. Directed by Emile Ardolino: Vestron Pictures, Great American Films Ltd Partnership, 1987.

Diski, Chloe. "Mark Ballas and Julianne Hough—Dancers." *The Observer*, March 3, 2002. http://www.observer.co.uk/osm/story/0,6903,658940,00.html (accessed March 3, 2002).

Dollar Mambo. Directed by Paul Leduc. Mexico/Panama: Programa Doble, 1993.

DVD/Authority. Review of *Burn the Floor*. http://www.dvdverdict.com/reviews/burnthefloor.php (accessed March 31, 2004).

Dyer, Richard. *White*. New York: Routledge, 1997.

Ebert, Roger. Review of *Shall We Dance?* *Chicago Sun-Times*, October 15, 2004. http://www.rogerebert.suntimes.com/apps/pbcs.dlll/article?AID=/20041014/REVIEWS/40921008/1023 (accessed March 21, 2004).

———. Review of *Strictly Ballroom*. *Chicago Sun-Times*, March 26, 1999. http://www.rogerebert.suntimes.com/apps/pbcs.dlll/article?AID=/19930226/REVIEWS/302260302/1023 (accessed March 16, 2004).

———. Review of *Tango*. *Chicago Sun-Times*, http://www.rogerebert.suntimes.com/apps/pbcs.dlll/article?AID=/19990326/REVIEWS/903260306/1023 (accessed March 21, 2004).

Farnell, Brenda M. "Ethno-Graphics and the Moving Body." *Man. New Series* 29 (1994): 929–974.

Feder-Kane, Abigail M. "A Radiant Smile from the Lovely Lady: Overdetermined Femininity in 'Ladies' Figure Skating." In *Reading Sport: Critical Essays on Power and Representation*, ed. Susan Birrell and Mary G. McDonald, 206–233. Boston: Northeastern University Press, 2000.

Fraser, Jill. "Let's Dance. It's Great Sport." *Herald Sun*, December 7, 2001.

Freedman, Diane. "Wife, Widow, Woman: Roles of an Anthropologist in a Transylvanian Village." In *Women in the Field: Anthropological Experiences*, ed. Peggy Golde. Berkeley: University of California Press, 1968.

Getting to Know You (also known as *Getting to Know All About You*). Directed by Lisanne Skyler. Hollywood, CA: Search Party Films, 1999.

Gillespie, Eleaner Ringel. "I Didn't Have the Time of My Life and I Don't Think You Will, Either." Cox News Service. http://www.accessAtlanta.com (accessed March 16, 2004).

Gottschild, Brenda Dixon. "Some Thoughts on Choreographing History." In *Meaning in Motion: New Cultural Studies in Dance*, ed. Jane C. Desmond, 167–177. Durham, N.C.: Duke University Press, 1997.

———. *Waltzing in the Dark: African American Vaudeville and Race Politics in the Swing Era*. New York: St. Martin's Press, 2002.

"GTV DanceSport." GoodLife TV Network. http://www.goodtv.com/program.php?programid=80 (accessed June 1, 2002).

Gurevitch, Zali. "The Tongue's Break Dance: Theory, Poetry, and the Critical Body." *The Sociological Quarterly* 40 (1999): 525–542.

Gustin, Marene, and Heather Wisner. "DanceSport Scores Big on ESPN." *DanceMagazine*, March 2000. http://www.findarticles.com/cf_dls/m1083/3_74/59870972/print.jhtml (accessed April 26, 2004).

Hanna, Judith Lynne. "Movements Toward Understanding Humans Through the Anthropological Study of Dance." *Current Anthropology* 20 (1979): 313–339.

Hawkins, Christopher, and Hazel Newberry. "Chris and Hazel's Olympic Dream." http://www.danceuniverse.co.kr/news/hawkins.htm (accessed April 26, 2004).

Herbison-Evans, Don. "Dancing in the Olympics 2000 Closing Ceremony." http://www-staff.mcs.uts.edu.au/~don/pubs/olympics.html (accessed June 1, 2002).

Hoffman, Max. Review of *Strictly Ballroom*. Internet Movie Data Base, 1992. http://www.imdb.com/Reviews/17/1744 (accessed March 24, 2004).

Hong, Yap Koon. "Guys, Here's a Modest, Important Step Towards a Sporting Centre." *The Strait Times.* March 4, 2002. http://straitstimes.asia1.com.sg/columnist/0,1886,300-78539,00.html and http://www.dancescape.com/info/index.html (accessed June 1, 2002).

Horton Fraleigh, Sondra. *Dance and the Lived Body: A Descriptive Aesthetics.* Pittsburgh: University of Pittsburgh Press, 1996.

Howe, Desson. Review of *Strictly Ballroom. Washington Post,* February 26, 1993. http://washingtonpost.com/wp-srv/style/longterm/movies/vide (accessed March 31, 2004).

Hubert, Rudi. "DanceSport to the Olympics in 1999." http://www.idsf.net/press99/games.htm (accessed March 2, 2004).

Hunt, Evan. Review of *Strictly Ballroom.* The Web, 1992. http://www.imdb.com/Reviews/18/1862 (accessed March 24, 2004).

Hunter, Stephen. Review of *Shall We Dance? Washington Post Critic's Corner.* October 15, 2004. http://www.washingtonpost.com/wpsrv/style/longterm/movies/videos/shallwedance.htm (accessed March 21, 2004).

"Interview with Hawkins & Newberry." *Dance Universe.* http://www.dancersplanet.com/, cited in http://www.danceuniverse.co.kr/news/hawkins.htm (accessed February 27, 2004).

Fraser, Jim. "Is DanceSport a 'Sport'?" *Canadian Amateur DanceSport Association.* http://www.dancesport.ca/cada/more/content/dancesport_a_sport.html (accessed June 1, 2004).

Jackson, Michael. *Paths Toward a Clearing: Radical Empiricism and Ethnographic Inquiry.* Bloomington, IN: Indiana University Press, 1989.

Jonas, Gerald. *Dancing: The Pleasure, Power and Art of Movement.* New York: Harry N. Abrams, 1992.

Karten, Harvey S. Review of *Dirty Dancing: Havana Nights.* Rec.arts.movies.reviews (newsgroup); de.rec.film.kritiken (for German reviews), 2004. http://www.imdb.com/Reviews/371/37158 (accessed March 16, 2004).

Kempley, Rita. Review of *Strictly Ballroom. Washington Post,* February 26, 1993. http://www.washingtonpost.com/wp-srv/style/longtermmovies/vide.

Knight, Tim. Review of *Dirty Dancing: Havana Nights.* Reel.com. http://reel.printthis.clickability.com/pt/cpt?action=cpt&title=Dirty+Danc (accessed March 16, 2004).

Koestler, Arthur. *Insight and Outlook: An Inquiry into the Common Foundations of Science, Art and Social Ethics.* New York: MacMillan, 1949.

———. *The Ghost in the Machine.* New York: MacMillan, 1967.

———. *Janus: A Summing Up.* London: Hutchinson, 1978.

Langer, Susanne. "Virtual Powers." In *What Is Dance?,* ed. Roger Copeland and Marshall Cohen, 30–31. Oxford and New York: Oxford University Press, 1983.

Leeper, Mark R. Review of *Strictly Ballroom.* Rec.arts.movies.reviews (newsgroup); de.rec.film.kritiken (for German reviews), 1992. http://www.imdb.com/Reviews/18/1861 (accessed March 16, 2004).

Lidz, Franz. "Dancing in the Garden." *Sports Illustrated,* September 27, 1999), 76.

Long, Daniel. "Qualifying for Olympic Status: The Process and Implications for Competitive Ballroom Dance." Master's thesis, Brigham Young University, 1999.

"Look Out Olympics . . . Here Comes Dancesport." http://web.uvic.ca/akeller/e240/Mag/mageg/dancing.html (accessed June 1, 2002).

Lucas, John A. *Future of the Olympic Games*. Champagne, IL: Human Kinetics Books, 1992.

Lugones, Maria. "On Borderlands/La Frontera: An Interpretative Essay." *Hypatia* 7 (1992): 31–37.

Macnab, Geoffrey. Review of *Tango. Sight and Sound*. British Film Institute, August 1999. http://www.bfi.org.uk/sightandsound/reviews/details.php?id=179 (accessed March 31, 2004).

Mad About Mambo. Directed by John Forte. Phoenix, AZ: First City Featured; Phoenix Pictures, Plurabella Films, 2000.

"Make a Date with Dance." *Dispatch Online*, September 15, 2000. http://www.dispatch.co.za/2000/09/15/features/DANCE.HTM (accessed April 26, 2004).

Malnig, Julie. *Dancing Till Dawn: A Century of Exhibition Dance*. Reprint, New York: New York University Press, 1995.

Marilyn Hotchkiss' Ballroom Dancing and Charm School. Directed by Randall Miller. USA: Carousel Films, 1990.

Marx, Eric. "In Ballroom, A Redefinition of 'Couple.'" *New York Times*, July 14, 2004. http://query.nytimes.com/gst/abstract.html?res=FB0B15F9345F0C778DDDAE0894DC404482 (accessed September 4, 2004).

Matthews, Tom. Review of *Dirty Dancing. Boxoffice Online Reviews*, September 1987. http://www.boxoffice.com/scripts/fiw.ddl?GetReview&where=Name&terms=DIRTY+DA (accessed March 21, 2004).

McDonagh, Don. *Martha Graham*. New York: Popular Library (Praeger), 1973.

McMains, Juliet E. "Brownface: Representations of Latin-ness in DanceSport." *Dance Research Journal* 33, no. 2 (winter 2001/2002): 57, 59.

———. "Race, Class, and Gender in the American DanceSport Industry." PhD diss., University of California, 2003.

Meyer, Carla. "Learning from Señor Swayze: 'Dirty Dancing' Transported from Catskills to Cuba." *San Francisco Chronicle*, February 27, 2004. http://sfgate.com/cgibin/article.cgi?file=/c/a/2004/02/27/DDG9058G6N1.DTL (accessed March 16, 2004).

Munzeer, Delerine. "Footwork Presents DanceSport 2001 Championships." *Sunday Observer*, February 18, 2001.

Nathan, Joanna. "Dance, Billiards or Boules—What Next for the Olympics?" CNN.com, September 24, 2000. http://www.cnn.com/2000/WORLD/europe/09/21/olympics.newsports/ (accessed April 26, 2004).

Ness, Sally Ann. *Body, Movement and Culture: Kinesthetic and Visual Symbolism in a Philippine Community*. Philadelphia: University of Pennsylvania Press, 1992.

Nichols, Stuart. "Is Ballroom Dancing A Sport? This One Man Says So." Outsports.com. http://www.outsports.com/letters/dancesport20011012.htm (accessed January 23, 2004).

Nochimson, Martha P. *Screen Couple Chemistry: The Power of 2.* Austin: University of Texas Press, 2002.

The Object of My Affection. Directed by Nicholas Hytner. Hollywood, CA: Twentieth Century Fox, 1998.

O'Connor, Sean. "Feel the Rhythm of the Music." *The Teacher,* June 2001. http://www.teacher.co.za/200106/01- sport.html.

Parkes, Brian. "Ballroom Dancing, a Gentle Sport?" http://www.dancesport.|v/eng/fun/articles/isdance.htm (accessed June 1, 2002).

Patrick, K. C. "Orphans and Olympians." *Dance Magazine,* February 2002. http://www.findarticles.com/cf_0/m1083/2_76/82322492/print.jhtml (accessed February 25, 2004).

Perelman, Chaim. *The Realm of Rhetoric.* Notre Dame, IN: University of Notre Dame Press, 1982.

Perelman, Chaim, and Lucie Olbrechts-Tyteca. *The New Rhetoric: A Treatise on Argumentation.* Notre Dame, IN: University of Notre Dame Press, 1969.

Peters, Sally. "From Eroticism to Transcendence: Ballroom Dance and the Female Body." In *The Female Body: Figures, Styles, Speculations,* ed. Laurence Goldstein, 149–154. Ann Arbor: University of Michigan Press, 1994.

Picart, Caroline Joan S. "Dance as Forms of Space, Embodiment and Culture." *Korea Times,* February 17, 1993.

———. "Dancing Through Different Worlds: Virtual Emotions and the Gendered Body in Ballroom Dance." *Qualitative Inquiry* 8, no. 3 (June 2002): 347–358.

Polier, Alexandra, "New Form of Ballroom Dancing Leaves Ginger Rogers in the Dust." *Columbia News Service,* May 8, 2002. http://www.jrn.columbia.edu/studentwork/cns/2002-05-08/604.asp (accessed May 8, 2002).

Porter, William. "Competitive Dancers Having a Ball." *Denver Post,* January 27, 2002). http://denverPost.com (accessed April 26, 2004).

Rangel, Castillo. "Athleticism in Dancing." 2000. http://www.webspawner.com/users/udsc/atheletism.html (accessed April 26, 2004).

Raven, Nell. "Taking a Few Steps to Fitness." *Edinburgh Evening News,* October 24, 2003. http://www.edinburghnews.com/print.cfm?id=1173712003&referringtemplate=http%3A%2 (accessed January 24, 2004).

Reynolds, John Lawrence. *Ballroom Dancing: The Romance, Rhythm and Style.* San Diego: Advanced Global Distribution, 1998.

Rhodes, Steve. Review of *Dirty Dancing.* Rec.arts.movies.reviews (newsgroup); de.rec.film.kritiken (for German reviews), 1987. http://www.imdb.com/Reviews/97/9736 (accessed March 21, 2004).

———. Review of *Shall We Dansu?* Rec.arts.movies.reviews (newsgroup); de.rec.film.kritiken (for German reviews), 1997. http://www.imdb.com/Reviews/84/8463 (accessed March 21, 2004).

"RSG: Art and Sport?" The Contortion Home Page, January 30, 1998. http://www.contortionhomepage.com/rsg_essay.html (accessed April 26, 2004).

Russo, Mary. *The Female Grotesque: Risk, Excess and Modernity.* New York: Routledge, 1994.

"Samba, Rumba and Gold." *Maclean's,* April 27, 1998, 12.

Savigliano, Marta. *Tango: The Political Economy of Passion.* Boulder, CO: Westview Press, 1994.

Savoy, David, and Sharon Savoy. "An Uplifting Experience at the Olympics." *Dance Magazine,* January 2001, 72.

Schulgasser, Barbara. "Accept This Invitation to the Dance." *San Francisco Examiner,* August 21, 1998. Originally printed by the *Hearst Examiner.* http://www.sfgate.com/cgi-bin/article.cgi?file=/e/a/1998/0821/WEEKEND15528.DTL&TYP (accessed March 21, 2004).

Shall We Dansu? (Shall We Dance?) Directed by Masayuki Suo. Japan: Altamira Pictures, 1996.

Sharp, Jasper. Review of *Shall We Dance?* Midnight Eye: The Latest and Best in Japanese Cinema. http://www.midnighteye.com/reviews/shallwed.shtml (accessed March 21, 2004).

Short, Norman. Review of *Burn the Floor. DVD Review,* 2000. http://www.rottentomatoes.com/click/movie-1094642/reviews.php?critic=all&sortby=default&page=1&rid=198006 (accessed March 31, 2004).

Sista Dansen (The Last Dance). Directed by Colin Natley. Denmark/Sweden/Norway: Eurimages: Metrone Productions, 1993.

Stern, Carrie. "*Shall We Dance*?: The Participant as Performer/Spectator in Ballroom Dancing." PhD diss., New York University, 1999.

Strictly Ballroom. Directed by Baz Luhrmann. Australia: Australia Film Finance Corporation, 1993.

Stoller, Paul. *Sensuous Scholarship.* Philadelphia: University of Pennsylvania Press, 1997.

———. *The Taste of Ethnographic Things: The Senses in Anthropology.* Philadelphia: University of Pennsylvania Press, 1989.

Swift, E. M. "Calling Arthur Murray: Ballroom Dancing Has as Much Right to Be in the Olympics as, Say Rhythm Gymnastics." *Sports Illustrated,* April 24, 1995.

Swing Kids. Directed by Thomas Carter. USA: Barrandor Studios/Buena Vista Home Entertainment, Buena Vista Distribution Company, 1993.

Tango Bar. Directed by Marcos Zurinaga. Argentina/Puerto Rico: Beco Films; Zaga Films, 1998.

The Tango Lesson. Directed by Sally Potter. U.K./Argentina/France/Japan/Germany: Adventure Films, 1997.

Tatara, Paul. " 'Shall We Dance' a Graceful Tale of Middle Age Yearnings." *Showbiz,* July 19, 1997. http://www.cnn.com/SHOWBIZ/9707/19/review.shall.dance/index.html (accessed July 19, 1997).

Taylor, Julie. *Paper Tangos.* Durham, NC: Duke University Press, 1998.

"The Sole Saver." http://www.thesolesaver.com/.

Topper, Susanne. *Astaire and Rogers.* New York: Nordon Publications, 1976.

Truex, Dorothy A. *The Twenty Million Dollar Give-Away: An Exposé of Competitive Ballroom Dancing.* Philadelphia: Xlibris Corporation, 2001.

United States Amateur Ballroom Dancers Association, Northern California Chapter. *Spectator's Guide to Amateur Dance Competition.* http://www.usabda-norcal.org/guide.html (accessed February 26, 2004).

Watts, David. "Love of Sport Takes a High Dive." 1998. Cited in "RSG: Art and Sport?" http://www.contortionhomepage.com/rsg_essay.html (accessed April 26, 2004).

"What is DanceSport?" *Genesis DanceSport.* Imagine Designs Studio, 2001. http://www.genesisdancesport.com/articles/articles_2001.htm (accessed April 26, 2004).

Williams, Jonathan. Review of *The Tango Lesson.* Rec.arts.movies.reviews (newsgroup); de.rec.film.kritiken (for German reviews), 1998. http://www.imdb.com/Reviews/110/11075 (accessed March 21, 2004).

Wynne, Colm. DanceSportIreland.org, April 1993. http://www.dancesportireland.org/features.htm.

Index